MER

MOM EGG REVIEW

Vol. 21

2023

Half Shell Press
New York

MER - ***Mom Egg Review*** is an annual collection of poetry, fiction, creative prose, and art by and about mothers and motherhood.

www.MERliterary.com

Front Cover Image: Jeff Rivers, "On the Phone," acrylic oil stick fabric on paper.

MER - *Mom Egg Review* is a member of the Community of Literary Magazines and Presses.

This publication has been made possible, in part, by a grants program of the New York State Council on the Arts, a state arts agency, and the Community of Literary Magazines and Presses. MER is grateful for this generous support.

MER thanks The Motherhood Foundation, *The Mom Egg* founding publishers, Joy Rose and Mamapalooza, and founding editor Alana Ruben Free.

MER - *Mom Egg Review* can be purchased directly from the press on our website, through online retailers, at select independent bookstores, and through EBSCO.

Contact MER at themomegg@gmail.com for info about discounts for quantity purchases and for classroom use.

ISBN: 978-0-9915107-9-5
(Half Shell Press)

Mom Egg Review
Half Shell Press
PO Box 9037
Bardonia, NY 10954

www.merliterary.com
www.facebook.com/merliterary
www.instagram.com/merliterary
Twitter: @merliterary
Contact: themomegg@gmail.com

MER

MOM EGG REVIEW

Vol. 21 - 2023

EDITORS' NOTES

The works, poetry, fiction, and prose, in this year's MER, our 21st annual issue, remind me of the movie that won the Best Picture Oscar this year, "Everything Everywhere All at Once." In it, a middle-aged woman has to wrangle an aging parent, a contentious teenage daughter, a failing marriage, and business and economic woes—all while saving the multiverse. Basically, what many mothers do.

And what the poets and writers in this issue write about. Spanning ages and stages, the normal and the surreal, the introspective and activist, these works explore, inside and out, the writers' personal experiences of motherhood, and the way that interacts with other aspects of their personhood, and with the world.

We live in "interesting" times, where cant, slogans, and snark are part of everyday discourse. The writing in this volume is the opposite—considered, nuanced, intelligent, questioning. Whether you read it straight through, or dip in throughout a busy day, the works of art and writing in this issue will provoke thought, identification, and perhaps, enlightenment.

Marjorie Tesser
Editor-in-Chief

As we were assembling MER 21, we were struck by the way the poems moved from the interior to the exterior; from inside the home to outside; from within the body to release. In her poem, "Questions for my Aging Body," Jennifer Edwards asks, "Why knock on the dollhouse door." The poems in this issue approach and enter that house, then move beyond it, where we are instructed by Kyle Potvin to "Locate a fragrant nut on the other side. And run, run for your life."

These poems are on a trajectory and ask us over and over: *who were we? who are we now?* In her poem, "At The Entrance To My Childhood There Is A Photograph," Lisa Bledsoe describes an interiority of the home and the body,

> I have not yet been revised—
> still the shape of my mother's lap, still
> made of sidewalk and toast and hardcover books.

Many of the poems are written from this vantage point of the mother and the mother seeing themselves as an *idea*, not fully developed. Jessica Purdy, in her prose poem, "Visitor," confesses, "I'm still imagining what a good parent does these days." Like a developing photo—or any metamorphoses—the poems masterfully describe this frenetic process. Sandra Fees, in her poem, "Don't," writes

> I began to recognize the shape she'd become—
>
> a Rorschach of branches and wings,
> a sacrum splayed, a whorled
>
> curtain trying to hold
> the breeze.

These poems of transition, that bring us to an outer place, do not shy away from the fear and pain involved. Meghan Sterling's "Self Portrait with Sparrow Song," transforms this necessary aspect of change into fire and song:

> Song of the sparrow, the wren,
> their voices blue as the ash of all your years set to burn.
> Song of your old life set free by the new.

The poetry in MER 21 honors and celebrates movement, within and outside the confines of the body and the home. The poems pay homage to what frightens us, what challenges us, and in the end, brings us to the place Dayna Patterson describes as having, “No regret. Love—a perfect pearl, a wine-sunk moon, a goblet’s O.”

Jennifer Martelli and Cindy Veach
Poetry Editors

CONTENTS

I. INSIDE

Art

Poetry

Nonfiction

Fiction

II. TRANSITION (MOVEMENT)

Art

Poetry

Fiction

Nonfiction

Fiction

III. OUTSIDE

Art

Poetry

Fiction

Nonfiction

MOM EGG REVIEW

Vol. 21 - 2023

I. INSIDE

Loretta Oleck - The Blossoming

Ariane Dreyfus
(translated by Elaine Terranova)

Inside

Since water goes everywhere suffering is like it

It enters the kitchen
The little boy has put his cup on the floor
Next to the dog where he sets himself down to pet it

Neither of them saying anything

One lying on its side the other nestling beside it
Leaning his forehead there,

"You're tired, Darling?"

It is the dog who looks up, wags its tail. When it rests its head
On its crossed paws, it keeps beating its tail against the floor
Like a good girl

At the sound, the child she thought asleep bursts out laughing. From below,
His little fingers manage to intertwine with hers.

She looks all around, everything coming back to her

The faded flowers
Of the oilcloth so often wiped
The red and green squares
Of the apron thrown over the chair
The open jar the gleaming jam

When she looks down the dog
Is ardently licking the child's temple

Why did she believe their days would stop?

Jessica Femiani

Frenetic

I think I was thirty-nine, the first time I wrote this poem.

At thirty-four the tick was just beginning to get loud; kind of like that first pound in the chest right when a panic comes on.

In the back of Convivium Osteria on 5th Avenue, I sit at a wooden table with my sister, my mother, and my father; we sit amidst large pots of decorative clayware.

My mother announces my cousin's wife is expecting, that she is just a few months along, and I burst into tears.

My mother, my father, my sister, with eyes tender, wait 'til I find calm.

Back then, even at thirty-seven, I still had so much time.

In my early thirties when I should've been having babies, all I wanted was to read poems.

I'd take the B/D to West 4th, climb down the narrow steps of the Cornelia Street Café, the basement theater's spotlight blinding my eyes, smudging faces in the periphery.

To speak my words, to let them fall from my mouth has been an awakening of sorts, grounding me in the wake of a newfound visibility.

Days later the words pulse through me, travel the course of my body, the patters of language enlivening, burning the back of my throat.

The tenured male professor sitting a row behind me, gloats news of his children, a grandchild, his grandchildren.

To think, I did this for poetry, poetry, my love, I've been thinking I want to be a race car driver, tires gripping curves tight, driving fast.

Glenis Redmond

Setting the Table

Mama hands me fork, spoon and knife
as she circles the table I follow her lead.
Learn *what comes around goes around.*
She demonstrates how to fold the napkins
and where the drinking glasses go.
I never ask her how she knows how to set a table
I just accept this as one of my many chores:
learning place and how everything has one.
I note how the table sits in the center of our home,
the place where mama's voice is the loudest.
Dressed with each and every season
Her table boasts Royal Dalton,
specifically the Country Rose pattern.
She collects eight place settings
any unlikely piece: salt and pepper shaker, gravy boat etc...
Mama doles out stories sparingly, but always tells me:
I'll never clean for white people.
She places this mantra deep within me.
In her eighties I learn why: *Mrs. Mary Burton,*
the woman whose house her mama cleaned
the house that loomed on the hill in Waterloo,
"Bring Jeanette," grandma was in no position to say no
so mama always came along as her mama scrubbed,
dusted, mopped, washed clothes and swept.
Mrs. Mary Burton taught mama place:
how to properly set a table.
How to polish the silverware.
Her mama's eye was on how her daughter
was being groomed, to serve. *What comes around goes around.*
She ships mama to the next county
where colored children can get an education,
Fountain Inn Negro High School.
Mama felt like unwanted hand me downs.
Given to her Aunt Carrie and Uncle Willie,
but her mama was giving her
what she never received, a chance.
In home economics mama excels.
Mrs. McDuffie marvels at how she sets a table,
gives her the highest marks in the class.
Mama parlays her skills as an Air Force wife
at woman's auxiliaries or church functions.

She becomes the go-to person at every base.
People look to her. When she looks at me she hands me
what she learned: how the table is the center,
what comes around is what she gives: stretched dollars
and a hand out to help me climb the ladder
to be the first in the family
to earn a college degree; *what goes around*
learning how I can go beyond what's set before me.

Joan Kwon Glass

Lamentation of a Mother at Mid-Life

after Camille Guthrie

I'm sitting at the dentist with my 15-year old daughter who hates me.
She has six cavities, and I have failed again as a mother.
All those years of standing at the bathroom sink with a timer,
making her brush for two minutes, and she still
inherited my tendency toward rot.
My fitness coach reminds me to drink more water,
says that it will help me feel full. But when I'm hydrated,
I have to pee every thirty minutes.
When I tell my 25-year old gynecologist this, she nods,
smiles cheerfully, assures me: *at your age this is perfectly normal.*
My ex still hasn't paid his half of the last dentist bill,
and ironically, I'm the one my daughter can't stand,
the one who, she says with a sneer, *does that poetry stuff,*
as if it's the silliest thing ever, as if it makes me a bad mother
to be good at something, to love anything besides her.
The other night, when she asked me to watch a movie,
I was hopeful that we'd turned a corner, until
she said: *I chose this because it's dad's girlfriend's favorite.*
Raising my daughter differently, fervently pursuing
that closeness I didn't experience with my own mother,
has gotten me nowhere different–the foundation I built
with mother-daughter journals, lessons and trips,
nightly reading and snuggle sessions–none of it was as powerful
as her inherited determination to be nothing like her mother.
Before I leave this office, let's warn the young moms,
so when they get to where we are now, they aren't so jaded.
They should know, that no matter our best intentions & long devotions,
desperate prayers that their fevers will break–our daughters may reject us.
Hopefully just for a while, but maybe forever.
This morning I noticed that the skin on my neck
is starting to resemble beige taffy stretched too thin.
I don't wish for the life of my younger self,
but I do miss her neck and bladder.
Wouldn't mind less fat under my arms either, though my friend
Naomi says armpit fat just means we will grow wings one day,
a sort of conciliatory evolution.
Let's try hot yoga, share the names of our favorite Vitamin C creams,
burn away our skin at the spa to reveal something new.
Let's decide to care less what our daughters think of us,
drink gallons of water until we're convinced we are full.

Jennifer R. Edwards

Questions for My Aging Body

after Eduardo C. Corral

Is there a mixed drink you don't like
Why knock on the dollhouse door
Do you require medication
Can't you stop questioning
Is it that you don't want your kids to grow
Can you even imagine yourself as an old lady
Why does beauty sometimes scare you
Were you OK, even for a second, with hands on your neck
Why did you want someone else's husband
Can you read without a pen in your hand
Will you ever embrace technology
Why does your heart thump on interstates
Do you think that much of this was justified
Are you still jealous about your mom's fingernails
Why did your dad teach you ice fishing
How many funerals will you miss
Isn't that deer carrying a message
Why are you always using teeth

M.P. Carver

Present Participle

Watching Cutthroat Kitchen
In my friend's living room
Cat sitting and at ease but
Thinking about the Supreme
Court deciding about a near
Continent of bodies, sea to shining,
Under the water, under the wet seething
Of the tides where I'm wearing my organs
Outside of myself, an ongoing issue
They're all talking about, incessant
Battling of the public stone titans
In the image of Jesus remembering
Suddenly that He is the son of God
When coming inside Mary Magdalene
Who is really the one I want to be writing
My poem about and, Mary, I'm asking
Honestly, if they're going to forget you
Otherwise why are you caring about them
Calling you a whore? He may have died
But just once, and not for you or for me.

Carrie Bennett

[Memory Box 1]

You're in a hospital room with your newborn daughter pressed to your skin. The year only three days old. You have no idea that China just landed a spacecraft on the far side of the Moon that never faces earth. You are a particle in a hospital robe. A 5-inch incision smeared across your abdomen. The word fear hibernates deep like an anchor speared into sand. In India two women enter a forbidden Hindu temple. How this can somehow dirty a space. Somewhere else the NRA sues over bans on semiautomatics. The hospital walls hold you and your daughter. You didn't discover anything to arrive here. Your body built another body as though each cell were a marching band. The moon contained in the long window overlooking a river— the evening already plummeting down. The word shame removed from your body for now. Watch your hands dissolve. And all the women who have cared for you. Your daughter turns into the most intricate snail. Never forget you don't deserve this.

Jennifer Pons

Mother of the Reluctant

At fourteen, my mother was put on a bus
to Minneapolis with fifty dollars and a lunch.
She went to a stranger's home
to buy an abortion kit in a paper sack
for her mother. They were both named Mary.
My grandmother had green eyes.
I have green eyes too.

At first, my stepmother's name was Mary,
but she changed her name to become someone else
she came to know living inside of her.
Once, she lost her baby. She told the story
many times. She didn't want to live,
but the doctors saved her. The baby died.
My stepmother said she crossed over
and back again in a new skin, with a new god.
I imagine her drowning in a river,
then flipping her body like a salmon
instinctively jumping to the surface to rid
the sea lice from her scales. She didn't like me
because I reminded her of my mother.
My mother was a lot like sea lice.
My stepmother was a lot like a lost baby.
I have always longed to become a new body
in a mountain river.

The naming of all three of us is a mistake.
I can't sort the mother part.
I think, at times, I am not supposed to do this.
The Marys didn't want to,
but I don't want to be like the Marys.
How does a woman escape inside the skin?
How can a woman repair the naming in the body?
My thoughts can't fit into a paper sack.

No woman can be Mother to the Shells.
Mother to Bus-Riders. Mother to Green.
I needed Mary the Girl who wanted
to be Mother of the Lonely.
I needed a mother before I became a mother.

Some mothers arrive without knowing.
Some mothers refuse. Some say
I am not a good mother.
Some have the grief of dying salmon
and dead babies inside. Some
wear the shape of mother
body-shaping babies who become
the bearers of shells and scales.

KateLynn Hibbard

If grief were a scar

I would never stop picking at it. It is a wound, it is wound around all of my days. I will not stop noticing her body there/not there, an emptiness filled, not filled. At her funeral, the church ladies told me she was proud of me. At her funeral, my queer lover and I were forced to sit behind my sister, her lawfully-wedded husband, her children. Who really knows the heart of their mother? My mother's body is in mine, her shape is mine, her arthritis is mine, her devotion is mine, her mystery, mine. I wore her winter coat a full year after she died. At her funeral, I turned away briefly and the lid clicked shut, that satisfying sound. And the body was finally gone. And the body is never gone.

Shannon Elizabeth Hardwick

Mercy Mother

The thing about losing, then wanting
something, like a ring, a book,

a T-shirt that once belonged to a grocery store clerk
who was also my one-night
stand, like a special

on avocados
that feel right for the exact time
I anticipate wanting them

and maybe I was right
to walk away—it takes a whole body

and then the absence of a body
to understand an empty bowl—

when sleep returns, a mother forgets
how any stranger's baby can make milk
appear—

pull a mouth away from what it wants and
it's a mercy for the mother if she decides early enough.

The mouth always knows—

about losing—at the same time
I'm not walking away; I'm searching for pardon.

Tina Kelley

To My Children, Out of the House

I love you two with the locked jaw of mad dog,
as fiercely as the rusty swing set loves
its thrush-note sighs.

My devotion to your protection has turned me
into a word that should not exist, an *écorché*,
a body stripped of its skin, a flay figure.

And if two-year-old you came back quick, racing
around the core of the house, livingroomhallkitchendiningroom,
smearing fudge on each wall and chair, I would rejoice. I really would.

It is incomprehensible to me now: I can go to bed knowing
you're about to board a plane, and I sleep all night
and you text at seven a.m. that you landed.

Be gone from you, embarrassment of dog in hand-knit hat.
Away, trifling friends, sadness of limping star forward.
May you never be the bad parent in someone's memoir.

My shield, my sword, here. I love you more than my calming
pulse, which has been such good company to me.
"I love you 20, 30, gigantic, tons pounds,"

as one of you once said to me, making me love you more,
love you with the swirly dance of the swim-tendrilled cuttlefish,
with fervor enough, perhaps, to make you keep being, ever.

Laura Goldin

Family

Mother excused herself again
        and went into the bedroom.
To put on her face, she said,

        Meaning the bright red lipstick
all the mothers wore at night, the powdered
blush they called rouge,
        and the lashes that resembled caterpillars
on the black enamel tray.

She had a set of brushes, like they all did.
Cases that clicked open
        and snapped shut, a
space beside her on the bench
where a child could sit and watch,
        dreaming of transformation,
learning things.

        Children did not have faces then.
And Father had
only the one he always wore,
        too big for putting on and taking off again.

On Wednesdays,
        in the afternoon,
Mother paid bills at the small wooden desk,
while I arranged myself,
        curled in the circle that the sun made
on her bed, and slept.

        So many years since then,
such waiting for
those long, still
        Wednesday afternoons,

Mother unruffled
        in the early summer heat,
the warm breeze that touched both of us
her moving pen
her open window.

Claire Keyes

Für Elise

Sing, my mother urged her daughters. *Play the piano.*
Be happy. Sitting on the couch, apron smoothed,
she waits for me to play Für Elise. Aunt Jo joins her.
I can't stay long, she whispers.

I like twirling on the stool. All year, I've taken lessons
from Sister Cecilia at the convent and my mother has heard me
practice. I feel loved and worth the two dollars she finds
in the sugar bowl where she keeps her stash.
Though I'm not ready, and will never be ready,
I will myself to play well, to make her happy.

She's warned her girls not to frown as she does, pointing
to the line creasing her forehead. If only I can forget
how shy I am, the notes will roll smoothly
as if Beethoven himself were my teacher.

My mom listens, and my aunt, both smiling as they rise,
bow and waltz around the living room, my mother's feet
suddenly light in their white shoes with the poke in the toe.

If it ends like this, I'm dreaming.

Mary Bonina

The Living Room

I knew my baby's hunger,
reading his cry, different from others:
tired, wet, bored, or sick with a cold.

Alone with him, I drove off road
and down a dirt path. I parked,
unbuttoned my blouse and only

then did I realize where we were:
in a cemetery surrounded by granite
headstones and potted flowers,

some dried up and frozen, others
perky plastic. Nothing flourishing
on a cold winter day. But I was there

nursing my boy, a few months old,
warmed by the car heater; the engine
kept running until he was satisfied.

And suddenly I remembered being
a child learning loss, how I turned
away passing cemeteries in the car,

and walking, I crossed the street
to the other side. I guess I thought
it was a way to ward off death.

I was a superstitious child, also
innocent enough to think I had power
to change the course of nature.

Was this the wishful or magical thinking
of a child who lived in fear after
a classmate's mother died giving birth?

I went to the wake in the family home
couldn't stop thinking after,
my friend had to live in that house,

where the lifeless body of her mother
was on display in the living room.
I thought of this that day with my son,

in the car as I fed him that afternoon,
when life—the opposite scenario—
was being played out in the cemetery.

Subhaga Crystal Bacon

Mother's Braid

In her fear that after her death, we'd have
to clean up after her—
        a strand of turquoise chunks
        all the family photos
        a garnet bracelet, bound in ten-carat
        gold, with matching earrings
        sent to her by her mother
        from Germany.

Also:
        softening skin between chin and neck,
        impatience, her hands,
        and a crooked spine
        from which hooked parts
        ache and need   to be replaced.

Mother/life/memory, a braid like the one
she saved
        from her own hair, the one
        she wore wrapped around her head
        in Bavaria, cut off when she came here
        to marry a near stranger at eighteen,
        nearly an adult.

Like the braid she never made for me,
my hair a continent she refused to explore—
        chopped short until the year
        I begged for and got a home
        perm to roll into a flip.

        Trying in high school on my own
        to curl my hair into something
        resembling a style, she told me
        I looked like—

How deep her fear of me
        all the ways I raised myself
        all the ways she tended me.

What she left, she gave me early.

Chloe Yelena Miller

Disarm

I was your home: your limbs nudged my bones to make room for yours.

Now in the dry world, you walk, even dance. I am no longer your walls, roof and floor, protecting your growth. This is how it should be.

I cannot save your body with mine if / when the shooter arrives. I cannot return to being your home if / when danger rushes in, knocks everything over.

You go to school to learn everything, like how parts make a whole and how your song and screams begin in your lungs with breath. No one can learn to be bulletproof, so you shouldn't have to try in the closet.

You deserve challenges you can fail at before trying again. Like building a bowl out of clay with two hands. If the walls collapse, you roll the clay into a ball between your palms, use your thumbs to build them up again. The clay may or may not become a bowl, but you can keep trying.

I cannot let you fail if / when the active shooter finds your classroom door, your desk covered in pencils and tiny erasers.

I must release you into the world so you can grow. This is how it should be.

And how it shouldn't be ~~if~~ / when …

Kimberly Ann Priest

How to Forgive the Predator

All living things must eat.
The stomach is not impartial; neither

the soul. We survive
by what we do and do not

nurture and sometimes this requires
teeth. I say to my son *don't incise*

the soft part of your heart. But,
he does, creating

a scar—each time toughening,
each time making the tissue

less susceptible to pain. When I got
divorced I learned quickly that this

is what made me desirable for eating,
having been broke down

by a mallet, my husband's
hammering anger tenderizing me.

Having forgotten pain.
Having learned not to squeal

in a cage but continue to release
the lactic acid that keeps the slaughter

from spoiling. My son
teaches himself to forget pain too

in the same house, on the same street,
with the same sort of fleshly

cravings, a little indifference
to break down his appetite for love.

Kevin Carey

How Much More Truth Can There Be

for my mom

This is the first place I go when I think of you: I was 10 or 11 and we sat in the Pewter Pot on the Legion highway and you showed me how to drink tea and we ate blueberry muffins and you listened as I went on about the movies or the Celtics, never in a hurry to close the conversation. And it wasn't you *trying* to be a good mom, it was you being interested, and loyal. You were always family first. Always in love with your husband and your children and your grandchildren, your refrigerator littered with newspaper clippings, photographs, crayon drawings, your family's business so unabashedly worn on your sleeve. What made me most sad in the end was how you would have seen yourself, no longer independent after all you'd lived through: your teenage days on the wild beach, the uncertainty of a Second World War, the death of your husband. You managed. And you found the good in so many simple things, even when the best parts of you started slipping away. I remember once sitting with you in the house on Lancaster Ave watching a re-run of *Bonanza.* You asked me if *Hoss Cartwright* wanted half of your sandwich. We both laughed when I said *he didn't look like he needed it.* You laughed easily. Yet you remained fierce when life hit back, determined to find grace where you could, and fierce when it came to your will to live. I was sure I saw you dying ten times over two years, my sister and I keeping a vigil in the patient's lounge at Salem Hospital. But you proved us wrong again. I was happy we finished that Robert Parker novel a few days before you died. It was called *Family Honor*, and the last line read, "Then I kissed him and closed my eyes, and the darkness was all there was." When I read it out loud to you (even though you were sleeping) I thought it was a fitting last line, the end of *your* story. Does it end? Today I believe you are walking hand in hand with your husband on some white sand beach, a piano and the drums being brushed, Nat King Cole crooning over the waves. It's the last scene in the greatest love story, the two of you walking into the setting sun, all of your life and all of your love surrounding you. It must be true because I once read a letter to you from your husband. It was sent from a base in San Diego before he shipped out in 1941. He wrote, "It will be a wonderful world when we can be together always." How much more truth can there be than that?

Rae Hoffman Jager

Perspective

Sometimes when I'm sad and want to feel like I'm in a smoky lounge drinking a vodka cranberry with lipstick on my teeth, waiting for a drag show to start, I power walk to Abba. Find distance from myself. With earbuds in, I pull my daughter behind me in a red wagon, and she falls asleep slumped over—dreams of her past life crossing the frontier in a covered wagon or remembers being dragged half-dead on top of other bodies mid-Dark Ages. That's perspective. Two people walk the same path— past the same dozens of brick houses— and see different rooves, grass, skyline. It's a matter of focus. When we pass the wide lens view of Cincinnati, unobstructed by leaves, my daughter awakes and sees bridges. Three bridges, mommy. Three bridges. What she chooses to fixate on is important to her. I see white ramshackle shed. I see skyscrapers turning the sky into a cheap low thread count sheet. All the houses slowly leaning, some tumbling towards the water.

Lisa Creech Bledsoe

At The Entrance To My Childhood There Is A Photograph

I am smaller than the steps up to the door,
my dress is straight along my thighs
in the Kentucky heat. I'm not thinking anything
except that I belong here and also not here.

I have not yet been revised—
still the shape of my mother's lap, still
made of sidewalk and toast and hardcover books.
The little dress is olive, with orange print.

There are thousands of me, outleafing—
none have yet been folded back to grass.
No clocks have been invented
and the sun is all sugar and wax crayon.

I don't know the Dairy Queen yet.
There is no memory scarred into my knees.
My great-grandfather holds my hand

Jessica Purdy

Visitor

I can hear the tree workers next door chainsawing the old limbs. Even the shower can't drown it out. I stay in extra long. Today I need to burn the cold out of me. There's this knot in my throat as if I'm pinewood. There's this failing that can't be swallowed. I've been remembering old facts of my childhood. Things that haven't stayed in fashion. Crocheted ponchos. My mother's punch bowl and a ladle for serving. The bundt pan ice disk floating like a lifesaver in a miniature pool. The sweet bubbles she concocted. I'm looking at my daughter's chaotic bedroom thinking I could make it into art. Her body I'm responsible for assembling is neat as a pin. Sharp contrast to her crumpled clothing mixed in with garbage. How she numbs herself against the knife edge of life. I'm remembering my father rolling a newspaper and lighting the kindling in the fireplace. His shoehorn and tin of brown Kiwi shoe polish. His tie collection. My mom's grid method for transferring an image. Carbon paper. Her green speckled case of pencils. I'm imagining what a good parent does these days. I turn away from the mildewed ceiling. Let the hot water pelt my eyes. Wonder why this balled up fist showed up today on the doorstep of my throat. I recognize the feeling. Its fingerprints clenched, a fist inside like a trees' concentric rings.

Kimberly Ramos

Reflection, But Shuffled

When night slips into my bed and once again / the world is a place with no edges / I remember you are my first homeland / You, Missouri girl of cattle and birthing seasons / you of barn cats kept for utility but naming them anyways / you of early morning chores when the sky is nothing but a flush of purple dust in the pasture / You, the body that housed my body / our blood meeting like tributaries / we flowed into one another / My dreams were your dreams / : / dark, senseless, fitful / Your dreams were mine / : / knee-high grass buoyed with Queen Anne's lace / dragonflies nose-diving at the pond / country fairs, cotton candy spooled larger than your head /

You, the white lady / ferrying around her Asian baby / us an oddity / a paradox housed in every pore / People asked / : / Is she adopted / ? / People asked / : / Are you the nanny / ? / As if your body / could not bear a body like mine / a body of squid-ink hair, cavernous eyes, barely-there brows / Mama, we were dammed from each other / We were sent / to separate purgatories / forever thirsting / for water / for what was / the ocean of us /

Mama, when I count the teeth in a room / it is because I have to / Can you blame me for believing / everyone wants to eat me / ? / It was something I learned on my own / after too many close calls / Mama, there is more than one way I can be gutted / more than one position / men want me to sin in / and even now, I find it hard / to sin for myself / Mama, for all your warm fur / I was always going to be part feathergirl / flighty, prone to wandering / searching / migrating /

But Mama / you always leave the porchlight on / and like a lighthouse / you burn so I can find you / Mama, the older I get / the more people say I look like you / and I hope that's true / our lumpy knees / homegrown hips / the thready stream of song / that escapes from our lips / and our loss for words / in the face of disaster / Mama, I know there are so many other things to be / besides being pretty / but thank you for saying / that I am / for loving what is you / and what is not you / and what came from the earth / and what is not of this earth at all

Mama, I am your reflection / but shuffled / with salt and sequins stirred in / O Mama, tell them / we came from each other first

Anaïs La Rocca

The Age of Oxygen

Sometimes I can't breathe. Sit up straight, they say. That'll make it better. Go outside; it's a nice day out. I've never had good posture, though I can fake it when I sense a camera pointing at me. And I've never liked reclining on outdoor patio furniture— though I know 'cool girls' do. Instead, I lie horizontally on my left side for hours absolutely drowning in Law & Order SVU reruns. Suffocating myself with fistfuls of Twizzlers.

I was raised in a city with very little sky. Not breathing should be nothing new to me. The New York City sky was a puzzle of blue slot machine rectangles rotating above us. Sky was the negative space where skyscrapers weren't. There wasn't much fresh air. But between the concrete corners and the margins of the city sidewalks, even without air, we found things to inhale.

Summer nights in the city were a dream. We climbed out of our tenement walk-ups. I slammed the door behind us. Outside, the air was sticky with cocaine, collapsed dust from 9/11, and cannoli sugar. We wore it like a layer of clothing. Kabuki make-up. And pinned against the brick walls we'd suck it off each other's teenage necks in the middle of the night— like starved animals given a saltlick.

By morning there'd be no more music, just the smell of hotdog water hanging in the air. The turquoise heels I stole from DSW would be a little shorter, hanging off my fingers instead of my toes. But for now they were still painless on my feet. I took a deep breath and lit a cigarette.

The ground up recycled glass within the pavement sparkled under our feet as we walked under streetlamps. The car headlights spotlit our legs against a blacktop that sure looked as if it were littered with diamonds and glitter. Who knew that crushing mountains of used mixed-colored glass and recycling it into glassphalt could create a landscape so beautiful. Sure, light pollution turned the entire night sky into a stagnant grey pond over our heads, but all the stars were at our feet— oceans of constellations we could walk on.

Those nights were half my lifetime ago now. I can still hear them. Now, years later, I can barely move from this couch. I feel crushed. I lie on my left side because I am told that if I lie any other way my vena cava will be compressed and I could faint, or at the very least, get a little nauseous. I think I'd prefer to faint. This constant neural feed of Olivia Benson talking to 'special victims' is a type of black-out drunk in and of itself. A lobotomy of illegal sex and crime.

At 34 weeks pregnant, I am told that my uterus is so large that it's crushing my diaphragm. But not to worry, this is normal. Life is crushing. I feel crushed by my own weight. I wish I could fly. I wish I could feel a strong wind current under my body, that gulp of air. I want to be waterboarded with oxygen. Inflate like a cartoon blowfish.

Today, we have the most air on Earth we will ever have. Yesterday we had a little more. Tomorrow we will have a little less. I consciously peel open each corner of my lung with my breath. I'd prefer this little girl on the opposite wall of my body, in my arms instead of abdomen. In about six weeks, she'll be evicted. She'll learn to breathe. We'll both inhale deeply for as long as we can, though life is short. At least half of Earth's oxygen comes from the ocean, an incredible idea, given that underwater is the one place we cannot breathe or live.

Kelley Engelbrecht

House Poor II

There is a thin sharp line inside my mouth, below my lip. When I put my finger in my mouth to press against the porous ridge, it smarts. My finger feels like a lump of chew, tucked into the pocket of my lip. I like how bulbous my mouth looks. Misshapen. I can't remember where the cut came from—perhaps it's finally gum rot—but I pass hours rubbing my tongue on the tenderness where it stings until it feels good. In addition to sucking my cheek, she started putting her hands in my mouth. She lies on her side, suckling, a long stare into the wall, her arm extended, waving around until her hand finds the softness of my lips. She uncurls a fist and stuffs, one by one, her small fingers into the wet cavity of my mouth. Her nails graze my gums. She pulls down until my bottom teeth are exposed, a thread of saliva drips.

The three of us lie in bed. I've curved my body in a soft arch around her as her gums search for my breast. The early morning static is hypnotic. She moves like molded Jell-o, leading with her feet from side to side, grabs the pink skin next to my nipple before turning away to grab his stubbled chin. We pretend to sleep but my body feels too precise— a leg over a leg so I can't roll over; an arm over an arm to barricade the pillow. In the softness of our center, she is finally still, arms outstretched, but I feel her looking into the exhalation of dawn's first blush. The ocular leitmotif of day brushes against my suspended cage made of blood and spittle. I hold both and neither: specter and flesh.The bathroom door moans. It cries as it heaves itself shut, slowly lowering itself into the belly of a penny-tiled floor. I wonder who has died here. Who has died here, what blood this house holds. What sweat licks the plaster walls, what cells layered underneath slabs. A house is wood and wall and roof and window but also overstretched tendons and body odor and a can of Old Style left in the fridge and a Federal Express box from 1988. Is it an A flat that slowly turns out of tune, the bathroom door, I mean. I remember the time that my mother sat in Gare de Bordeaux-Saint-Jean until she figured out that the signal for an incoming train was a perfect fourth by singing "Here Comes the Bride." Or was it "Amazing Grace"?

In the hush of an early spring night, the baby is sick. We scoop her up, pajamas hanging off her body, and bring her into the bathroom where I've been running the hot water, drumming up steam. The night light has a red bulb. It flickers. The three of us: my husband holding my child. My hand on her back, my hand on his arm, we sit in the steam, in the red light, hoping the mucus will dislodge. We start swaying, my husband holding my child. My hand on her back, my hand on his arm. Our hips move to a stream of water hitting our porcelain bathtub, in steam, in red light. Our bodies breath together, swelling and constricting, in and out, in and out, in and out. Sway sway sway sway sway sway sway sway sway sway sway sway sway sway sway sway.

Tessa Ellison Rossi

Five

Two is there on the blanket, and now Three. Three is leaking from his swim trunks-over-pool diaper. Three is two, still untrained, hopefully leaking only chlorinated water. Four has made you an expert in triage. Three says offhandedly, "My body makes its own chocolate." You cross your fingers, sniff, exhale.

Plonk! One! One is atop the grassy knoll, sniping acorns down at napping Four. You will kill him. One wants all the attention, *always*, a first/only. Two scratches in the dirt beside the blanket, talks in parables to Three. One sidles down the hill, traversing, squirrelly. Three watches Two, fascinated. His mouth moves, forming silent letters. Three is two but already knows his alphabet like friends. His toys have been boxed up for the house staging for months, all except the refrigerator magnet alphabets, upper and lower case. Three is a third, makes do with what's available. What One allows him. Three never gets to hold the controller, which is just as well. Sometimes they give him one when the batteries die and he beams, believes he's been accepted, and One smirks. Always smirking, that one. One snatches the stick from Two who mumbles dejection, squats beside Three. Best to defer. One begins tracing letters. "What letter is this?" "C," blurts Two. "Duh," says One, "I'm asking *him*, Genius!" "C," says Three, confident now. "And this one?" "A!" Three nearly drools in anticipation. In this way, Three is like the family dog. Also, he pees sometimes on the floor, and is loyal to a fault. So forgiving, your Three. He's a love puppy. "CAT!" "Not so fast, bro." One adds a curve with a kick to the scratchings. "Oh," says Three, "*R*. That's *car*."

You make sure Four is still asleep and there aren't any ants crawling on her in the stroller. You wish it reclined further, but it's the down-market version from the now-bankrupt toy conglomerate, and Four is the caboose. Four's bare foot rests atop the front bar and you drape your damp towel from the hood ever-so-gently so she doesn't sunburn. One is scratching furiously in the dirt and Two is scratching his head and you've positioned yourself between the boys, the carriage, and the water and so delude yourself that a moment is possible. You pick up a book. The letters wriggle and dance on the page in the glare. You look at the clock on the snack bar. Quarter to four. You really need the restroom. You're desperate to remove the soggy nursing pads from your wet bathing suit but you've draped the Discretion Towel on Four's stroller. The pads are irritating your nipples still exquisitely sore from Four's first tooth. The cotton is cold and lumpy and you can't imagine how much your body in its ill-fitting suit must appear like a nightmare to the two teenage lifeguards guarding the kiddie pool. Who you imagine glare at you hard through their mirrored lenses because you're the only family in this section and the sole reason they can't take a break to check social media on their phones.

"Um," pipes Two, "I don't think that's such a good--" "Shut up," whispers One to Two. "I'm giving him a harder word now. He can handle it." And to Three: "Sound it out. You're smart. You've got this!" *To Three!* You're surprised and suddenly proud of One, who seems to be maturing a little, becoming nicer to the younger ones, the boy you remember.

You're thinking about how many minutes to go before you can give the Five-Minute Warning and corral them into a changing room. Dry pads, dry bra and underwear, moments away. Takeout pizza on the way home, a sleepy carful, early bedtime. Get the boys down and settle in with Four and the book. Three will hopefully not ask you again in the changing room (sincerely and loudly) why your boobs look so sad. Four's stroller begins to jiggle. The foot rises, slams down on the bar. Wailing rises. Your breasts start to tingle, then ache and milk runs down the inside of your bathing suit. You stand up, begin to gather their belongings, and step on a yellowjacket crawling unseen along the remains of Three's discarded cherry-lemon-flavored novelty ice pop that he dropped on the grass once One plucked the black gumball eyes from its grinning face. "FUCK!" cries Three, triumphant. *Absolutely,* you silently agree and cannot pack up fast enough to rush them out to the minivan.

II. TRANSITION (MOVEMENT)

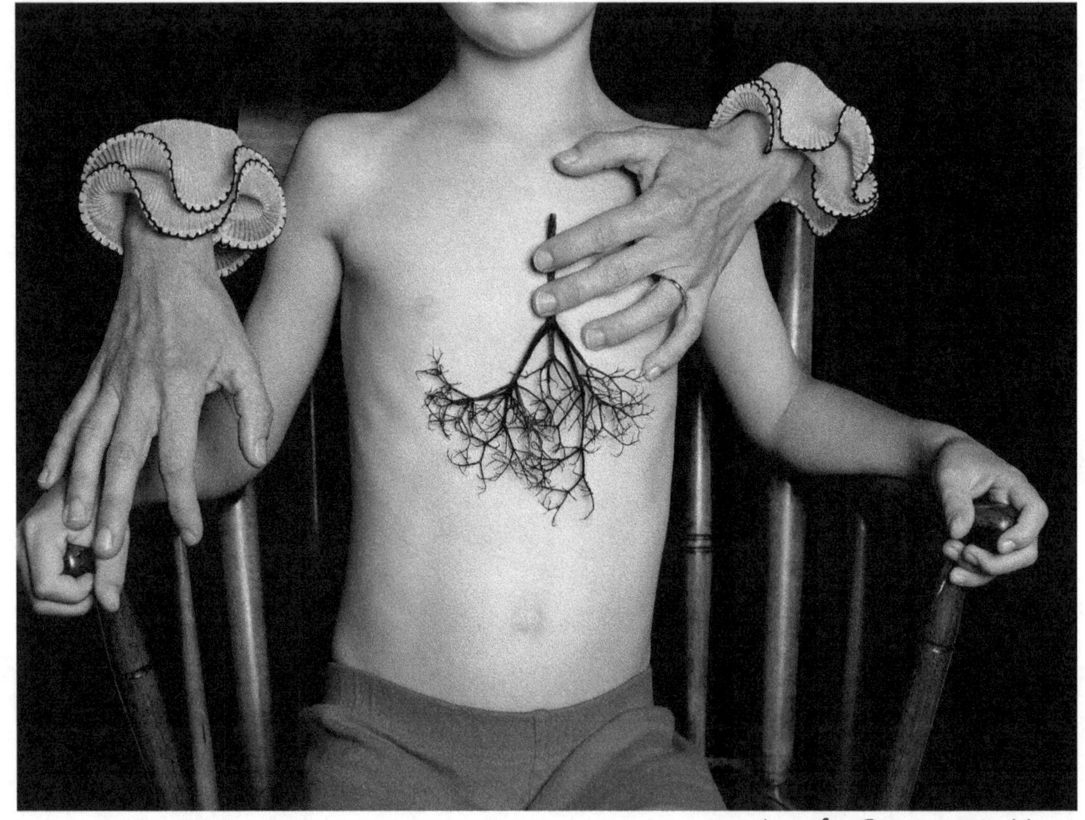

Jennifer Georgescu - Veins

Pat Hale

Lost

I lost my new poem about motherhood yesterday,
at the post office, here in town. Must have

stuffed it into the mailbox with the Christmas cards.
One minute I had it, and the next, it was gone.

It doesn't matter how true it was, how well
it stated all I wanted to say about wonder and distress

coexisting in one heart. Without an envelope,
it's just a scrap of paper going nowhere.

When I try to recreate it, my fingers are thick.
My words stumble. I'm distracted by sparrows

flittering on the lawn where last night's rain still pools;
by the way light defines color on the framing

of the porch door, how a single continuous panel
can be both bright white and dark gray,

at the same time, by virtue of how the sun
hits the roof's overhang. How boundaries shift

with time. How the wind passing through
the arborvitae branches can change everything.

Julia Kolchinsky Dasbach

Week 38: Leek

You've been leaking
for weeks now,
secreting, sieving,
seeping, sweating even
in the absence
of heat. You've been
leaving yourself
on every fabric,
spending more time
surrounded
by water
so what escapes
comes home.
You even asked
they check
it hasn't broken, asked
they test your liquids
against a colored strip
that shows PH and acid
or their lack,
to reassure you
Remy's ocean
isn't swelling
onto land. Each night,
your uterus contracts
as though she's just
about to come.
Each morning, she swirls
still inside. The sleep,
now heavier than log
or bone or even
death, more still
than sunken ship,
so when you wake,
your hip or inner thigh
is bruised from lack
of motion, your body's
pressing hard, its leaving
beads of self behind.

Anne Elezabeth Pluto

In My Church, Mary Wears Red

> The Moscow Patriarch had repeatedly bestowed blessings on the Russian military, giving a historical golden icon of the Virgin Mary to a senior commander, for example, and casting the war as a holy struggle to protect Russia from what he called Western scourges like gay pride parades. He has been a vocal supporter of President Vladimir V. Putin, with the church receiving vast financial resources in return. – Neil MacFarquhar and Sophia Kishkovsky, *New York Times* April 18, 2022

Let's take Her out of the picture.
Out of the historical golden frame
where She wouldn't stand
for being in the pocket of a general
scourge – the cold eastern blame
of the west. She sees the exchange
of gold and gems – what those who
do not have eternal life see fit
to deal with – let's take Her out
of this picture - She's left on a train
to the sea - She's standing in the graves
found in Bucha - She's wandering in
the steel plant in Mariupol – this Holy
Week – this Passover feast – this month
of fasting – She's covering her hair – her face –
She's opening her hands and reading
the central list of the dead – She's
stepping into the *Chorne more* *
swimming mermaid like her red garments
trailing the fishes and every broken mother's
wishes to pull the dead sailors to shore
in militias – to show – to show - their weeping
mothers – their blinded criminal country the cost
of lies – the cost of lives – and She rises
Venus like from the sea – Stella Maris -
Theotokos** – Mother of Jesus – announcing
the resurrection in this, the cruelest month
of the year.

*Ukrainian: Чорне море Romanized: *Chorne more*, IPA: [ˈtʃɔrnɛ ˈmɔrɛ]
** Greek: Mother of God

Marie Gauthier

Second of Three

Middle child, hinge child, bridge child
Child of self-soothing, sand sifting at the water's edge
Child of make-believe, of obduracy
Child who made himself an anchor
        lodged on the floor until his way was won
Tinker child, born scratching his big pumpkin head
        turning gears nearly audible
Child who could why us into oblivion
        and catch us in any lie
Child who raged when denied, raged until he cried
        crying the break in the lock
                the oil in the hinge
                        the secret in his heart's attic

Martha Silano

The Whole Vagina Experience

When I told my friend Hanita it was not a fun time
to be a mom, that the best I could hope for
was détente, not being told

I'd ruined my daughter's life. When I texted Hanita *she chewed me out*
for enrolling her in gymnastics! It's like PTSD, those goddamn
poxed and toxic coaches,

she texted back *shitty teenage years. It's what they do, their rite of passage.* It helped,
really helped, because lord knows I had my rite of shittage too,
telling my mother she'd fucked us all up,

insisting my siblings and I thrive in spite of their ad heck parenting,
telling her all of us have been shrinking on couches for decades,
checking ourselves into ashrams,

ohm-ing to undo the mess of their pieced-together-with-threats nest.
When she calms down, you should illustrate your birth to her.
The whole vagina experience, which took me back

to the hospital where I still walk the hallways, trying to spur on dilation.
I was at 2 cm, wanting to cry. Instead, I crawled on top
of a giant rubber ball, bounced for an hour.

3 cm. Damn. So I walked some more. Found, on the 5th floor, a red and yellow mangle
of a Deborah Butterfield horse. By 10 pm I'd gotten to 6! Not enough
to start pushing, but by one in the morning I could.

I pushed for over an hour. The midwife got close to my face:
You need to take a deep breath and push harder
than you've ever pushed in your life.

And then she was there. She was crying. She was gray and vernixed and bloody,
the cord having been wrapped around her neck. But she was on my chest.
They put her there before they cleaned her off, I think, to revive her.

Once she was pink, once it was clear she wasn't going to die, one of the two nurses
named Sharon bathed her, brought her back to me, so I could hold her,
so I could nurse her, so I could rest.

Annelies Zijderveld

Once I was a mother

Once I was a mother for 91 days. Now I am
a fly suspended in amber. A buzzing radio.
Cracked iPhone screen. I wear my mother
hood loosely, google "how to detach after" t
to see how autocorrect fills in the gaps. I am
aflutter to see his name on the missed calls.
Pause and then dial him without questioning,
listen as his messaging system isn't set up.
These are the days of dry lightning showers
that startle the night with all crack, no boom.
Overhead the helicopter circles as if surveying
me watering the plants before the blight of
powdery mildew, an all-probing eye in the sky.
What remains after fire burns it all down, the
ash becomes my ash. The dust, my dust. I hang
my address box on the rubble as if to make it right.
I go looking for him on Disney+. Close the door
to the room that at last begins to stink of sweetness.

Danielle Lemay

Broody Hen

The five hens cluck-dance when they see me
walking towards them. Their door flings open
and they race into the yard of their bug-dreams.

These fluffy orange hens shit white-green globs
under the blue sky. I sit in the middle of the yard
to give them another home base, like the coop,

the fence, and the canopy of citrus trees.
When they have pecked enough in one spot,
they waddle-run, little chicken herd, to another.

Their five-pointed combs stand tall atop
their heads like red mohawks, little
chicken weathervanes of health and happiness.

The last hen remains in a nesting box
each day, her comb ash-colored and limp:
If I don't sit on these eggs, who will?

What we will do for love—a few of us forget
to eat or sleep, chew our fingernails, fly
cross-country on red eyes for 36-hour

visits, we drain the last of our account, bail
for a son in jail, or we feed a child the milk of
our breasts, over and over, hollowing our bones.

We push ourselves too far like this hen
sitting still on a clutch of eggs
even while the ants crawl over her.

Merridawn Duckler

Still Life With Thrifted Object

I feel an affinity for the objects,
many hands touched and one hand
threw away. The discarded anniversary plate
after the adversaries have commenced.

Craps and edges, still cling, relieved of duties.
A jumble of unlike-colored items
that trash talk across eras
what it was to be exalted.

Even contraband was once up to some good.
The piece of the past missed in the present frenzy.
Beauty in uselessness. How a thing
needs to be moved to reveal a value.

The value in what moved us first.
I said to the dealer, look man, this glass,
improbably whole after crazing and contagion
a mother once filled, to satisfy a child's thirst.

Dayna Patterson

Gertrude on arte materna

An imperfect mother, what words can I say you'd be willing to hear? We give birth, love, fail to love. Deliver our children as stars to night's bleak-black mouth, knowing they will burn and burn out. Summer swallowed by bitter winter with no sun. Life's gift paired with grey pain, death. How terrible the knowledge: snow drifts on snow, no green growth beneath. How terrible the paralysis once the bones begin to roll. The foils clash. Pray you go first. Pray to the God of Lost Sons he will see your devotion at last. A final word: know the fierceness of your love will drive out fear, eclipse it complete. No regret. Love—a perfect pearl, a wine-sunk moon, a goblet's O.

Sandra Fees

Don't

I began to recognize the shape she'd become—

a Rorschach of branches and wings,
a sacrum splayed, a whorled

curtain trying to hold
the breeze.

René Magritte says, *We only perceive the world*

behind a curtain of semblance. I reached
for what no longer clung

to bone. Muslin filtered
morning to monotones

of ivory and eggshell. I recalled Mother

musing: *I suppose it isn't possible*
to live in two worlds.

But she did, for a while.
She was everywhere,

a river birch unscrolling a papery husk.

I couldn't contain her. Even a feather-
hand on her vein-thin body,

scolded away: *don't hold*
me down
don't—

Andrea Krause

Linea Nigra

The shaded line molts, obsolete
          calendar sloughs. Months

scrub rough. Penciled yardstick
          eraser dust. Stretched

muscles slump beneath,
          deflated into fresh

gorge. The river is running
          parched and fading. Cradled

in the sag. Resting
          as though it made an etch

into a fault. The chasm
          is elastic, attempting

to cinch up on its own. Canyons
          have opened up

elsewhere and I have slipped
          inside. A body

marked. Carved out.

Crystal Karlberg

In The New Year

My children scatter likes stones and all
of last year's accumulated knowledge

is already useless. *Extant* is a passive way
of saying we exist. Once I lost my car

in the airport parking lot. What is terminal
in Nature? What is the nature of illness?

You can bear a burden or bare your soul
with all the same letters, but arrangement

is everything. My mother knew about flowers,
how to bash their stems with the butt of a knife

to keep them drinking. Warm water is more
enticing to most people, though hot springs

in Kentucky offer bliss in winter. Even ignorance
isn't enough to keep the buffaloes in Turkey

from wading in up to their elbows. Something
about milk and later cheese, all reported by an eye-

witness. Words like *baby* get lost in translation
as if there's nothing left to say

when all we set out to do was heal old wounds. Not
new ones, that would be insane. I see the mystical

mammal in you. I bow down. I roll around. Impatient.
The oldest woman is now one hundred and

nineteen years old. When asked how she managed
to live so long, she said: *Family is so important.*

Melissa Joplin Higley

Bloodline

I traced the raised veins
on the top of your hand,

controlled the flow
of each blue-green line.

You were younger then,
than I am now.

My fingertip held
the current, created

a dam, then let go—
whoosh!—a river filled.

I couldn't wait to have hands
like that—that vascularity.

But, when those veins rose
on my smooth hands,

I resented their worming,
fragile bulges. (Everyone says

we look alike.) I pressed
my veins smooth again,

skin pulled taut, suspending
the flow a little less

each time, then let go—
I see how each dilating vein,

drooping eyelid, fledgling jowl
is a body's legacy, how

these ripenings will be all
I have left of you to touch.

Jennifer Barber

Writing Too Fast, I Write "Thew" for "The"

As if you and I commingled
                    in the dark and later the same day

I give birth to little baby Thew,
                    born in winter under a mauve sky.

By early spring he cuts a tooth.
                    He sprouts a curl. The yard's fescue

and crabgrass thicken, lapping up the sun.
                    Warm in my arms, little baby Thew

babbles his lips, laughing as he sees
                    a plane overhead, a dove on the roof

calling another on a branch.
                    He and I flow into you

like waves that slide across the sand
                    before sliding back, as they always do.

Suzanne Edison

Etymological Buckle

In the book of word origins I find—
To speed you on your way—my mother's
voluminous, cursive script parades
diagonally down the page.
To speed: from German*; to succeed or prosper.*

Her prescient words—laid down thirty years
ago, before I conceived this literary line, this
lineage of work—reveal themselves when I discard
the ripped dust-jacket.

Our discourse then? She listened
as I bragged my knowledge of our mutual
muse, Psyche—the storms once
buffeting, constraining our hearts
and minds, held a truce.

Now, my breath unbuckles.
Her blessing stands
like a shield's boss, an omphalos

begging me to align, bow to these tangled
roots, even as they surprise and sequester loss.

To lose: *be deprived of, or cease to have.*
Learning to speak, I cinched and loosened
my lips, repeated her words, hastening
towards my mother tongue.

Shoe, baby, door.
And, *today, I want, more.*
Please.

Deborah Bacharach

My Mother at the Husky Football Game

Today, I sit next to her trying
to pretend not to be bored.
When she leans forward, I follow
the purple and gold glow. Every year
for fifty years getting closer
and closer to the 50-yard line.
Every year, she spends
the big bucks, then more.

Thirty years ago in the divorce, Mom won the right
to this late afternoon, the sun as golden
as Henry Weinhard's Private Reserve.
She explains the touchback rule
as if I hadn't grown up
in this religion. I smile and nod
because she raised me to be kind.
When she offers the opera glasses,
I take them, watch for the snap,
but I miss it, am still sitting

when Mom jumps up, yells,
Get him! Get him!
She turns to me
breathless, laughing. She says, *I know*
you don't want to be here.
I say *No, I do. I really do.*

Pramila Venkateswaran

Women for Women

We're staying right here

we're not leaving even if planes are waiting to carry us

to a different country.

Why would we leave

uncertainty

to a different uncertainty?

You say we will be killed here.

Our lives have always been precarious.

A falling star was no falling star, for we became ash.

If we escape,

who will support the women who depend on us,

our daughters whose dreams are just beginning to sprout.

In this gnarled land of brown mountains

and houses pockmarked

with bullets, we are ships, our shawls buffeted by winds.

We've tasted iron and felt coarse voices of authority

sandpaper our skin.

Rules knife us into obedience. Maybe,

we know what to expect, or perhaps we don't

when we step into violent light.

We know our place is to make space
for our sisters, mothers, daughters, even if it means
breathing our last breath.

Our terms go unheard.
Our knell sounds clearly across our land, our beautiful,
relentless Afghanistan.

Tarisa A.M. Matsumoto

The Undertaker's Wife Waits Among the Dead at Lake View Cemetery, Seattle

Not everyone knows that a coffin and a casket
are not the same thing, not until they are smothered
with regret and second chances never given, a body
in cold storage, a body they used to know well,
though now even the color of hair is up for debate.

A casket and a coffin are not the same thing,
like a husband and an undertaker are not the same,
a right brain-left brain schism, tectonic plates drifting
and colliding, a Pangaea dissipating into the past and
the future, a border no one can fathom.

We look out over the lake, pioneers of this town
entombed high above it. Who would expect to find
an Orion and Narcissa among these petrified stones,
the occasional tree, dried grass turning the sky yellow?

Near the graves of Bruce Lee and Denise Levertov,
a young couple are buried deep, a monument rises
above them, a tear in the granite. They died
on the same day. No one asks why
the two halves of their marker are breaking
apart. What mysteries we will never unravel.

A casket and a coffin are not the same,
like a husband and an undertaker are not the same,
though they both carry the dead. We are different
bodies, we are different sides, and no one
will tell us why we break, no one will keep us
in the stars, no one will tell us why
we look for ourselves among the dead.

Debbie Koenig

You didn't ask for this.

Well, maybe you did, when you spent fifteen months failing to get pregnant, feeling your ovaries pucker and buckle like ancient apples forgotten in the crisper. When you injected yourself with hormones that made you cranky and uncomfortable and desperate, and peed on stick after stick, so many sticks, never seeing two lines. And when you found an article that described your experience so exactly you got angry, furious at the REs who never thought of endo, all those months of trying, trying, taking your temperature every morning, fucking at exactly the right moment, propping your legs up against the wall to keep his jiz, all those potential babies, inside you, ruining sex with your partner, maybe forever. All that time wasted when all you really needed was surgery.

All you really needed, as if it was nothing to track down the right specialist, to lay back, splayed and wincing, as a gyno surgeon stuck her hand up your vag, way way up inside you, feeling around as if she were digging through your sock drawer, while you prayed she'd deliver the good news: You were fixable. To do a euphemistic "bowel prep" the day before surgery, your partner administering an enema—emptying you out, killing any sexy feelings forever, maybe. Then surgery, which thank god you don't remember, and recovery, feeling razor blades move through your intestines. Which turned out to be gas.

And after all that, you fucked your husband one time, one time, it hurt too much to try for more, and two weeks later a second line appeared, a glorious miracle, you couldn't believe it, couldn't trust it, spent the next nine months waiting for some cataclysm to hit. But it didn't, you had a flawless, unexciting pregnancy, your partner doodling speech bubbles out of your swollen belly button, singing to the baby inside you, his cheek against your belly, the stubble prickly and intimate on your skin. Delivery so unremarkable you can barely remember it. You had a baby.

And every day since, you wondered why you thought you wanted this.

Thousands of days, wondering why you thought a baby might be the thing that would repair you, would make you normal, calm, oh-sure-whatever, when of course motherhood only made you more anxious, convinced that somehow you could get it right while every day you got it wrong. If you could just conquer thrush or colic or sleep training or finding a preschool or birthday parties (so many birthday parties, then fewer, then none) or chaperoning every class trip in second grade or keeping cool when the vice principal summons you or crying with relief at high school graduation or any fucking thing, just get something right, then your kid wouldn't be that kid, the one who holes up in his room, wandering through virtual labyrinths of white supremacy and misogyny, the one who marches with tiki torches, who sports a 1488 tattoo you Googled after that one time you caught a glimpse, a tattoo that keeps you up at night.

Until one day texts barrage your phone, links to tweets, news alerts, grainy photos, each one peeling back more of your skin, and you don't know if it's him, don't know if it matters.

It could be him. It could be. You might have gotten everything as wrong as it could possibly be.

Marie Harris

The Ring

It might as well never have happened, so distant are the wide church steps, the organ chords, the wedding party. And Marina.

That night in 1962, in a dingy room in a third-class hotel in Paris, all I wanted was for Bill to forget that girl we'd left behind in Norway.

Back home a few weeks, I missed my period. I went to a gynecologist I found in the phone book. I had never been to one before. And yes, I was pregnant. I needed a doctor's name. And I needed money. My aunt gave me the name. My high school friend, Marina, came with me to the pawn shop where I sold my mother's charm bracelet, two pairs of earrings and the precious gold signet ring I had been given for my sixteenth birthday.

It was early morning when Bill and I arrived at the office on New York's Upper West Side for the appointment. The waiting room was crowded with sick people. A woman with her cranky child. A young man with a bruise on his cheek and his arm in a sling. I read a magazine. The old man opposite me did not read. There were more women with children. More young men with wounds. Name after name was called off. Never my name. Hours passed. Bill grew restless. I dozed off. We didn't dare ask a question. Finally, as the light was leaving the windows and the skyscrapers began to glimmer, I was summoned into the doctor's office.

A small man, he sat behind a large dark desk cluttered with framed color photographs of his family. He asked me if I really wanted to do what I had come to do. In response, I pushed five one hundred dollar bills across the desk and began to cry. He directed me into a windowless examining room and told me to wait.

Next thing I knew I was being hurried out into the hall toward the elevator, Bill's urgent voice at my ear hissing *Is it over? Is it over?* It seemed the doctor had taken my distress as a change of heart and dismissed us. It took until the ground floor for me to explain that no, it wasn't over, that nothing had happened, that I was crying because I was exhausted. So we went back up but now the doctor was angry and nervous. He said he'd come to my hotel in the morning. *Now get out of here, both of you!*

And the doctor did come, with his black house-call bag like the one my father always carried, to a hotel room not unlike the one in Paris, but without Bill who had disappeared for the day. There were some preparations. A shot. I helped him move two heavy, scratchy armchairs to the foot of the bed and he arranged my legs over them. I remember talking too much. I could see into the window across the street. A seamstress was working her sewing machine. Then a sudden pounding at the door. I'd forgotten I'd ordered a sandwich. I started to call out that I wasn't hungry anymore, but the doctor signaled me me keep very still. The sandwich went away.

The phone rang from somewhere else in the city. *Is it over?* Yes, Bill, now it's finally over. Please bring me a box of Kotex. When he returned he said how embarrassed he'd been to have to buy it. He wanted sex. He felt, he said, lonely and ignored.

A year later I got pregnant again so this time we decided to marry. We were both finishing our sophomore years in college. He would continue on. My mother worried that her elegant fitted satin wedding dress would reveal my condition. She needn't have.

My father and I get out of the black limousine. He lingers, saying something to the driver and lighting a cigarette.

For a moment I am alone on the church steps. Into that moment appears Marina. She presses the gold signet ring into my gloved hand. I stare at it, barely recognizing my own initials. I bought it back, *she whispers as she slips it onto my finger.*

T*hen my father is at my elbow. Inside, the music begins. I continue up the stairs, with new misgivings, into my story, as though nothing had interrupted it.*

Barbara Lock

The Perpetual Devotion

If the man with the too-large feet seated next to her at the bar is her husband, he should be older, but his face is smooth and hairless, so it must be her son. She has trouble remembering what her son looks like now. Mouth always puckered and ready. This man here sucks at a pale, foamy beer. She smells smoke and sliced fruit. Through the full-height windows with a view of the street, another man—this one on a bright green, metal stepladder—prunes a pretty crabapple with a delicate chainsaw. The bartender moves a damp blue rag across the zinc countertop with quick, purposeful movements. That's three men to keep track of now—or is it four? She touches the left wrist of the man who might be her son.

"How are you coming along?" she asks. He shakes his head. The bartender wipes invisible crumbs from the counter, zip-zip. Everything in the restaurant except for the zinc countertop is bamboo lashed together with more bamboo. The walls are a stockade, the bartender a sentry on the top of a fort, polishing metal. The man who might be her son tastes the beer again, pouts.

"You were always such a particular child," she says.

"Paula," says the man, "I thought you wanted a celebration." His expression, a mirror of the one he wore when he tried to learn to nurse. (He failed—they both did. She'd tried to get him to suck the milk out of her breasts by putting a drop of sugar water on each nipple. This resulted in bitter crying and a raging case of thrush.)

"Cheers," says the boy, the man, without raising his glass.

"What are we celebrating?" she asks, and the bartender laughs. In the glass, a crabapple branch crashes to the ground. "What I'm trying to understand," she says, "is should I drink what you're drinking, or should I try something else?" Her son finishes off the pilsner, and the bartender disappears the beer glass underneath the counter. The bartender's hands radiate heat, and she knows that if she were to touch one of them accidentally (or on purpose) it would leave a permanent scar in the shape of a hand on her hand. From behind the bar the sharp sound of metal on metal. Or is it from outside?

The men had pretended to be soldiers at Fort Snelling—she was a girl on an outing with her mother and father, and the joke the pretend soldiers told had to do with shoes. (There were only two sizes: too big or too small.) The soldiers paced off in a courtyard, leveled their muskets, shot blue smoke over the prairie. A gray cat sitting on a rock didn't run away until she tried to feed it a pickle, then it gagged, glared at her, stalked off behind the stockade.

"I don't remember who you married," she says to her son; he looks much older now. Even from moments ago. He starts to cry, puts cash down on the bar. He is too old to be crying in public. He is an old man now! "Stop it," she hisses. She looks around the restaurant. No one is watching. "I thought I taught you better than that," she says anyway.

The bartender takes the cash from the bar with his glowing hand. She wants to interlace her fingers with it, to pull his hand close to her chest. She wants to rock the bartender in her arms, to feed him from her body, but she can't. The old man gets up from the bar. His feet are remarkably large, and he kicks the leg of a bamboo chair on his way to the door. "Pay attention to what's around you, young man," she says. Her boy likes to be told he's a man—they all do. Her boy shakes his head, wipes his eyes. "I told you to stop crying," she says.

"Let's go, Paula," he says. He taps the bamboo bar front with his fingers. "Stuff grows so quickly. That grove in our neighbor's backyard—Stan hacks at it daily," he says. She tries to see the old man's back yard with its encroaching bamboo patch, but it won't enter her mind.

Instead, she sees the green chair on a lawn where she once had a drink. Blue smoke drifted over the fresh-cut grass. The hard candy on her tongue was too big for her mouth.

Darlene Taylor

Road Chase

I wonder about the new woman. Ex-husbands tend to restore themselves in the bodies of younger women. After so many years knowing Vergis, I ask myself, *is he that kind of man*? I had imagined her tall, all legs. Long, freshly trimmed hair or maybe curls she runs her fingers through when something puzzles her.

She's none of those things.

Deep brown eyes peer through thick mascara. She smiles frosted-pink strips. How different she and I are. I'm broad where she's narrow. She seems too slight to lift moving boxes.

Verg didn't mention your coming, she says. Come inside. Warm up. She sounds earnest, but her face reminds me of the grimace on Noboy when the ice cream isn't the flavor he wanted.

The icebox-white room smells of garden blossoms, honeysuckle, and lilac. I feel anxious like when I used to sit on mama's front porch swing, secretly spying for Vergis, knowing that four o'clock he'd come, waving and grinning like he found a nickel, then whispering his plans. Country-living was too small for him. Mama came to the screen door, studied the overalls and dust-covered work boots Vergis wore, and decided he was no good. Birdie, your daddy be here soon. Come on inside. Vergis left, leaving his spell on me. That Vergis gonna chase roads, she said. Mud won't stick to his feet. He gonna keep moving 'til he done.

Later that night, he called at my window, face bloodied. I left with him.

Sorry for the mess, the new woman says. I scan the condo-living Vergis took on after saying he divorcing me. I fold myself onto the stiff couch as the new woman reclines into the chair I bought Vergis ten birthdays ago. Elbow on the chair arm, she rests her chin in her hand, crosses her legs. He'll be home soon.

I had practiced the things I would say. Noboy ain't blood, but he my child. I raised him. I lean back, hating the damp in my shoes and the curtainless windows. Streaks of red, blue, yellow, and green dabble. The city seems too close.

She places her hands where her blouse widens at her belly. She's pregnant. A half-smile appears. I'm glad we finally meet, she says. I've been thinking about Noboy.

He my boy.

Noboy needs his father. Words come easy from her. No ain't or sho nuf in her mouth. I bet she don't shout when she say please.

Noboy itching for roads he don't know about. Vergis ain't one to teach. Standing, I'm close to the recliner and long-ago spills the new woman can't see. Flashes of rum and coke blur into the rain-soaked trees over her shoulder. Vergis in that chair, drunk-eyed, red mean, belt over his knuckles. I don't shiver in front of the chair.

Noboy be best with me, I tell her.

It would mean so much to Vergis. He—

Best I be on my way.

She sighs an *I-tried* sigh and walks me to the foyer. At the door, she places a hand on my shoulder, and I feel the familiar tiredness of mending arguments.

Consider Noboy—

I stop her. Noboy my concern.

We are his family.

There's kinfolks and kinships, I say. You can't even clean stains off old corduroy. You got no way of knowing the road we come and seeing where it lead.

Vergis has a chance to be a new man. A hand slides to her belly.

Vergis would whip his past out Noboy. Whip the ain't out of him, and then he'll whip on you. The light behind her eyes won't let her see my way, so I go.

I cross the busy street ahead of horns and sirens. The city can eat. Have I been wrong for not telling Noboy that his blood mother left him at a make-do mother's door?

When Noboy does get home, he mumbles something about buses running slow, slouches at the kitchen counter, and hunches over a plate of peanut butter and rolls I make him. He switches on the television without considering if I want to watch. His half-turned face so much like Vergis, jutting jaw, long nose. He even stole his laugh from Vergis.

Pop makes hoagies.

His cooking must be something special. Never saw him do it.

I stretch my feet beneath the coffee table and recline to a solitary game of *Monopoly*. I shake the die and toss. Seven. I push the out-of-fashion boot.

Noboy bent over reminded me of Vergis after those boys beat him saying he raped their sister. Vergis ran that night, and I left with him. Months later a thin-faced woman came with a baby she couldn't care for. Leave the boy, I said, and he became my boy.

You fight with pop?

Takes two to argue.

You mad because pop got a new woman.

You looking and listening, but you don't see nothing.

The doorbell rings, Noboy opens the door, and Vergis comes in play-punching Noboy. I see broad muscles press against Noboy's t-shirt stripes. Vergis gives him a hoagie and some money. Go get two cokes.

Laughing, Noboy lands another punch and leaves.

Vergis comes at me with drunk-red eyes. I'm taking my boy back.

I can't have that. Vergis is angry. I know him angry, and he don't like me when he's angry. Since the new woman Vergis call himself *family man*. Noboy needs a steady head to keep him on the right path, I say. Your head low down.

I want my family whole, Vergis says. Things *I* got to teach my boy.

You gonna put a crib next to Noboy's bed? I shout. And what about that new woman? What Noboy gonna learn?

Vergis throws the hoagie at me just as Noboy returns. What's this? Noboy asks. He wipes mayonnaise off my face with his fingers.

Come on, boy, Vergis says.

Noboy squats, places the racecar on the game board, and rolls the dice.

III. OUTSIDE

Lauren Walke - As a Hen Gathers Her Chicks

Dorsía Smith Silva

Sunspotting

My body is a chart of white stars
awash in galaxies adorned with strings
of pearl clusters on my legs
and arms. A planet of infinite beams
seethed too close to the sun, abound
in white patches against brown rings.

Somewhere I like to think
there's my lost moonchild
circling in orbit. Maybe clustered
by my bellybutton
or spinning across my breasts.

I like to think that those tiny white
dots fed by ceaseless light
would tell me how to tether him,
the way a mother tells a child
tell me where it hurts
point to it: here, here.

Livia Meneghin

elegy in waiting

far into
the woods,
fallen logs,
overgrown
with fungi
threadlike
& bright,
die—

& closer,
spider webs
lie across
the heights
of violet
lilacs, while
early spring's
tulips linger
under high
noon, not
gone yet,
still too soon

inside,
a bouquet's
early bloom
shies from
wineblue
lights in
a white room

biding by
the back door,
a woman
tries to find
a lion's tooth
in a bowl
of basil
& time

Sarah Herrington

Tamarac

Car-o-Mat spelled backwards, a carwash in South Florida
owned by the same man who owns a country club
a deciduous North American larch
of moist soil
with short needlelike leaves
that turn yellow in fall
may refer to
settlements
wild areas in Minnesota
rivers in Minnesota
rivers of Quebec
or: a road in upstate New York with a Stewarts on one end
and feed store on the other, in the middle our family farm
a trailer park
a swamp, some of my teacher's homes
a strawberry farm and houses with windows that looked like eyes
land I could escape into to avoid all of them———-

There, I befriend calves pulled from their mothers
and get a taste for adoption
in a world that trades bodies for money
and bodies can be hurt or lucky
there's no telling the difference

Suddenly, I am six again
I put my fingers in the young calf 's mouth
she sucks thinking I have food, am mother

Abby E. Murray

Heirloom

I'm driving while talking
to my eight-year-old
about how even good
people can be jerks
sometimes and there's
a pause then she asks
from her booster seat
in the back
    but how come
        you've never
            been a jerk?
and the question is
a cluster of jewels I can
carry on my collarbone:
my daughter's belief
that I am too good
to ever be unkind,
because for her, in this
moment, on this day,
I am. Reader, I have plans
for this memory. Why not
take it home to save
for later, keep it in the box
beneath my bed until
the first time she swears
she hates me, her words
choking the house
like oily smoke? Then
I can dig through
my heirlooms for this,
the way she loved me
when she was eight
and I was incompatible
with fault. I'll fasten it
at the soft of my throat,
that well from which
countless wrong words
have sprung since before
she was born, and I'll shine,
if only for myself,
still visible in the dark.

Katie Hartsock

The Observation Artist

> . . . he is closer to things, since his eyes are only two or three feet from the ground, not five or six. Grass, stones, and insects are twice as near to him as they will be after he has grown up . . .
>
> from Edwin Muir, *An Autobiography*

He is so capable of stopping,
of holding the question that fits
in his hand, a flower desiccated.
His cheeks agree: it really is colder,
and familiar shapes browner,
more distant. Coming close
to the distance is what counts now.
Not so much the birds, today.
He knows the trees divide
with flashes, sometimes his mother
says, *Look!,* but the world is not
that high. He is the prairie path,
the variance of its borders.
Neither he nor his mother know
the names of their favorites.
She could look at her phone to look
them up: coreopsis and coneflower,
Joe Pye, wild rye, hoary vervain,
prairie sage, stiff tickseed—
but this is not their kind of looking.
They are watchmen not of names,
even wonderful ones. He trusts
such words enough to let them be.
Today his looking must be quiet.
Everything asks for quiet, except
his mother: *come on now, let's*
catch up. He walks slowly but still
more quickly than his looking would
like. Then the earth, long soft with grass,
changes into sandy soil! He feels it
through his shoes and stops to touch
the surprise, the recognition.

Anne Starling

Logic of Grief

1.

If I think I will see your four-year-old
self at the park, where we used to go so you
could run around in the fresh air & sunshine, back
when we had no backyard. If I think you'll
be there, and it won't take long to see you,
because though now we live in a different
place, that park is still the same distance
away—

Well, there's the rub, the logic
the stubborn saying nothing
is lost ever.

2.

I dreamed you were here, grown-up
as when you last came home,
and dreaming, I clutched your hand,
your arm, your side. This was a hug: so happily
I was hugging you, because how much
I had wanted to hold your feet, your hands.

That day, as I was making up your bed,
you offered to help, but I wanted to do it myself—
a kind of gift— so you stood watching, and what
you found to say was almost balm.

How you placed your hand on the top
of my head, gently, twice that morning
and once I reached up to touch
the top of yours.

Eileen Cleary

Leaves & Blooms

Soon, April. And those of us who'd frozen our fingers
clothespinning children's outfits into brightly colored popsicles,
or who'd shoveled snow just before the town's plow pushed
the icy streets onto our driveways, or who'd spilt the golden
retriever's ashes we'd agreed none of us would scatter until
spring when all of us could gather, blink away lopsided snowmen
blinded by hungry does. We notice the neighbors drag away
electric deer who've glared through our windows for so long
that our rescue puppy no longer interrogates them. We cannot
help but recall our parent's tree, its poisoned tinsel,
or the year Sheba swallowed it while large with litter. Or was that
the year she'd widened but didn't whelp, the year
she'd collected and mothered the ornaments,
the year she would not let any of us near the torn rabbit?
Anyway, their deer had stood since before the couple
left to have their daughter, and long after the morning they
returned without her. But, let's not fret about Christmas
decorations from our past, or those strewn on our neighbor's lawn.
Mud season arrives despite the stillborn, the earth rolling over
as predicted. If we live long enough, we pause
when the ground softens, the woodpile dampens
or the sparrow's song is close enough to touch.

Kyle Potvin

Upon Leaving: As Written in the Book of Squirrel

If you insist on exploring the heavy forest to the east
or the homesteads of the south, then travel quickly.
Directly. Do not stutter in your opening salvo
of leaving. You think you can turn back. Don't try.

I have ventured across wider streets than this.
Here I am. Others who tried are not. There are hawks,
snakes and foxes, and other things that crush a body and spirit.
But if you stay, you will be stifled by the monotony of limbs.

I am too old to leave this place where I know every bud and berry.
But you. I see your tail twitch with greed for the land
you glimpse but have yet to reach.

My little kit. Once I carried you, blind, for months. And now.
But this is not a story of millennia. This is only yours.
Someone once scoffed at my dream of joining a different scurry.
I went anyway. As you must.

Go. Nest in the crook of branches. Bury what you need for the cold
days ahead. One day you will remember what you need and dig.
Travel light. Remember how I taught you speed, distance, focus.
Eyes ahead. Light does not always illuminate.
Better to trust yourself in the black of night.
Locate a fragrant nut on the other side. And run, run for your life.

Lupita Eyde-Tucker

Self-Portrait with *Captains Courageous*

The tropical storm outside churns
like the hurdy-gurdy the Portuguese fisherman played
on night watch

when the sea was calm, the moon glinting
off the waves. Tonight, I'm forty-nine, feeling over swept,
lost at sea.

Time is a hand line fully unwound, hauling over
the gunwale. I'm hooked through like bait, jigged
along the bottom.

In the film, the father and son are two wreaths tossed
on the water, floating apart. The fisherman finds the boy
who fell overboard

in the fog. But, what more can he do? My children and I
are just like the boy, who tried to bribe his way
back to shore,

because all lost children want to be found
by a father. We're all treading water, desperate
for a rescue.

My children and I cry when the fisherman dies,
wrapped like a button shank fastened
to the sea,

and I'm hooked by his song played on a hurdy-gurdy—
it's all that keeps me from falling
into the fog.

Mary Lou Buschi

I Saw a Girl

Run in front
    of my car,
at a red light.

A man
    quickly after,
swatted the phone
    from her hand,
growled something
    I couldn't hear,
shouldered her back
    onto the sidewalk,
while another man held
    open the gate to a building.

I couldn't tell. I couldn't tell
    what their relationship was.
As she walked,
    head down,
protesting, I noticed
    her broken sandals.

As the light
    changed
convection waves
    blurred the row
houses across
    the street.

I couldn't tell her
    I know how impenetrable
male power is or
    how I wished
to give her my shoes
    made for running.

Brandel France de Bravo

Final Descent

After my mother died, I spent sunsets on the roof, scouring the clouds, white tea leaves in a drained and darkening cup. A few times, I thought I sensed her up there, lingering like the smell of her empty apartment: old paperbacks, tobacco, and *Miss Dior.* At once, a disembodied ear and the domed auditorium. How must it feel to be perpetually traversed by smooth-talking planes, satellites that repeat the same old stories? I have no religion, and still I'm a sucker for ascent. And yet, the sky is not the only vastness. *Listen, O Drop, give yourself up without regret/ and in exchange gain the Ocean.* Why not a candle lit by other candles in a cathedral of roots, or an orange blossom in the Alhambra of my heart? Call it failure of imagination, a reflexive craning towards the light. On top of our house by the airport, tracking a jet's descent, I imagine the passengers rehearsing for touch-down: what not to forget, who to call first, the psychic unbuckling. Another day that the door with glowing red letters did not open.

The night she died, she called to say she couldn't breathe. I had just left her bedside, after checking the plastic nozzles in her nose and kissing her good night. "I'm dying," said the voice on the phone. "If you're able to talk to me, you're still breathing," I laughed. And with that, she laughed, too, her oxygen sliding down like a window shade before a long flight. Undimmed, immune to the sleeping pill's effects, she was more herself than she'd been in months. "Terminal lucidity," they call it

Meghan Sterling

Self Portrait with Sparrow Song

Green fields leaning towards gray water
and the song in the underbrush just beyond
the tree line. You were bidden here. Song of the cedar branch,
song of the summer morning. Fan your feathers out
like your grandmother's Hermes scarf, a silk tail
of pink and brown squares. Follow it up the soft back
nearly broken by love. Song of the curtains closed to the sun.
Follow it to the place where the bus would drop you
along the road with its peepers, its trophy wives
and masturbators. Song of the squeaky bed. Follow it
across the atlas in a zig zag until you come to the man
in the ficus, his sex in his hands. Song of the runaway,
the memory housed in our shared bones. Follow it to the house
that would birth you. Song of your daughter, waking.
Taking your face in her hands like the moon at its fullest.
Follow it until you come back to this branch, heavy with summer,
light with needles about to drop. Song of the sparrow, the wren,
their voices blue as the ash of all your years set to burn.
Song of your old life set free by the new.

Elizabeth Garcia

Red Crayon on Paper, 2021

for Lydia

Her baby finger blossoms
the page, poppies unfolding

their tongues, their little roars
of origins, of all the bright

insides of us, the heart's
plump apple bulb,

its contained little shuddering
fruiting the body, ballooning it

past its own orbit, the way a rusty
planet is a theory of salvation,

one cardinal a theory of awe
or a bright cherry bead

a theory of your mother
how the flock of them clicked

in your baby mouth
as you sat in her lap, content,

fat with her scent. To know then,
her body, that first room, first surety

of place, would be to return,
to know it close to death, flushed

with brushstrokes, its canyon
a flame of sunrise—but oh! to be

again, tucked tight to her chest
still clotted with cream and strawberry.

Karen Elizabeth Sharpe

How I Shoplift

I check out invisibly.
Isolation rides invisibly
in the child's seat of my
cart heart.

I want my life back.
Even if I have to steal it.
I swipe one, take two:
Clorox, toothpaste, crosswords,
tape – not Scotch – a knock-off brand
to piece together scraps
of Addonizio's *What is this thing called love*
that my new shelter dog chewed up
because she got off the transport
van from North Carolina shivering
and chewing the way an addict
follows a familiar route of loneliness.

I refund myself in sweet potatoes
debit life of this pandemic
payback for time lost
for the grinding of my teeth at night
a cake for the birthday my daughter
had to celebrate alone.

Sunflower seeds, striped ones
for bluejays crowding my deck
bluejays which symbolize clear vision
or endurance, or safety, or protection
depending on which spirit guide
I google that day.

A bathing suit, sunblock
watermelon for the summer I missed
each skipped scanner swipe
swipe at the checkout
sweet soundless restitution.

Robin Gow

Beautiful Abortion of My Future Salamander

Overturning rocks in search of my offspring.
After a rain, the world soaked in bellies.
I was told I could be a vessel if I inhaled
everything the world wanted to steal from me.

On the news, I am told the butchers are being butchers.
I am told I once made a knife for them
and used the knife to pick my teeth. Looking at meat,
I always used to wonder where the blood went.

Crouching in a river of mothers, find her. Glossy
little apostrophe. She will soon want to be owned
or else flushed down a toilet like a goldfish. Googling
"what do babies eat?" and finding a recipe for veal.

No one will know of this though. When the river said,
"Empty yourself of amphibians." If womanhood were
a reservoir I could drain, I would spill the water
and fill it with fruit. Ripe nectarines and peaches.

This is when I was a human. When I split a cell in half
like a clementine. At the lobes and felt them grow legs
in my mouth. You were never here. Not at all.
"Yet" was a pair of lungs I used as socks.

Gloria Monaghan

Saturday's Child Works Hard for a Living

Shoveling the snow
a robin spoke to me
in the blizzard. Her rounded and tufted body
told me of her possible pregnancy and suffering.
Snow sat heavy in the pine.
My mind drifted into a space
of nonthought
like a knight on the road
on his horse sleeping and dreaming of nothing,
a red cross on his right shoulder.

Robert Carr

Words In Body and Stone

Needing proof of my survival, I tattoo rebellion in flesh, needle my mother's shame in ink – She also doubted her existence. A barb wrapped shoulder. Fist clenched, filled with a movie star kiss she tongued behind the moon, blue skies and a winged snake, self-doubt wrapped in cellophane. The bird on me has held her shape and I retire to a garden of raised beds. Grasses break frames in eyeglasses, tomatoes green to yellow on the vine. Grieving in a field, the child I was is shocked behind electric gates. He creates a simpler tattoo than my truth.

In this resting place, I carve my explanations in the headstone of my choosing. I write: The body is a flight through sternum. Mary, mother's name, carved in rock and deltoid – letters mossed in her confusion. She looks for answers beyond pursed lips. Earth hemorrhages like a September, and we all share a dark father with the light. Even now, a son names my shadows in graphite.

Beside the graves, the outline of my husband's hand, hieroglyph in relief, the long reach of his touch. Sometimes, I whisper, Hold me, in his ear. I'm done with being human – chiseling lost hours, flaking skin, a prayer for ink to fly. Promises are washed away in sandstone. I've never kept a secret, even Mom's. Heirlooms planted, I let the legends rot in light. I have a spotless agate in my barn.

Violeta Garcia-Mendoza

Cento Drawn from Conversations with My Younger Daughter

What? What?! Holy crackers—
babies are useless, tiny people!
I'm still in shock I can be stopped.

It's hard not having three hands
to help you. When holes have socks
part of your foot is cold. I get afraid.

The sun is alone. I caught the rain.

I used to think I never wanted
to go where there are bats.
Is this still America?

Why? Why though? What happens then?

Look at the sky. Don't touch it—
it's above us. Look—there's flasher-flies!
Tell me a story about clouds.

I'm so hungry I could eat my hair.
Toast isn't square; it's more heart-square.
Let's feast! Why should I not?

I'm making this day so much better
with my pterodactyl.

Margo Berdeshevsky

Songs

A lamb. Not lamb of god. My lamb. My crying all night and I'm telling you my everything friend. You have no name, dirty white fake curly fur soft enough to clutch in my paws and get wet with my

crying, lamb, confidante I hold in bed on the twelfth floor, ninety-sixth street Manhattan, water- tower-silhouettes like top-hatted golems watching me through the open shade. I can't sleep. My

mama's asleep in her room. My father's asleep in his room. My grandma died tonight — night. I tell you, lamb, my gramma's dead. It's long after dark. I tell you and tell you and tell you, Gramma with

black hair unbraided down to her knees, hair they chopped off when mama sent her to a nursing home in New Jersey where she died at dusk. I'm telling you, lamb, my gramma is dead, all

water-towers watching me night. I'm ten. Maybe I'm eleven. Once, my father cut off all my hair. My Gramma who has no down to her knees hair anymore is in her bed in a nursing home in New Jersey

and dead. — I'm a woman now. Not ten. Not eleven. No lamb. A woman of a certain age, aging badly, someone said, aging solo in a foreign bed. Three times divorced. Awake in the middle of a

night when news says war is beheading, is butchering, again. There are dead limbs of god and no lambs of god, there will be too many. I'm telling my animal. Telling my dead gramma, Telling my

now gone mama. Lost now, once-upon-mine lamb. Remember when gramma died and I held you all night? Remember how I felt for my once curls my father chopped off, fingers stroking your dirty

white pelt and whispering dead? Remember how you hissed something back to me in the no nightingales no sounds dark? What did you say, loved lost animal of mine just soft enough to hide in

my arm crooked between neck and the breasts I hadn't grown yet? What did you say to push me through that night like a needle? Songs of war are on our own steps now. Not there. Here. Here in our heads. In our breasts. On our steps. Everyone says so. Tomb steps. World steps. Woman in her bed tonight steps. Tell me—. I didn't know they were slices from poems like bits of skin. You told

me, *I am the tree that trembles and trembles.*[1] Told me a child who walked in bare-branched woods with her mother finding a small dead thing on the ground—how it was a Thanksgiving then and how she

told her mother, *I'll name it delicate.*[2] You told me *The quieter you become the more you are able to hear.*[3] Told me while I held my breath until the heart would stop. Told me poets could say such words. Right?

Lamb, tell me those again now and make me quiet. Right? Because tonight has to be the quietest night of my life.

---

1 *Muriel Rukekyser*
2 *Terry Blackhawk*
3 *Rumi*

Natalie Shaw Evjen

(Matre)synesthesia

My son was born without testicles. I didn't notice, partly because I'd grown up with four sisters, no brothers, and a ten o'clock curfew (I could count the number of penises I'd seen on one hand, including the Statue of David) and partly because I was still in shock. For nine months, I'd been brushing off pregnancy as a conspiracy theory. But here he was. My own miniature human.

It was my husband who learned of their absence first, from the L&D nurse squeezing opaque gel over our baby's eyelids.

"Testicles haven't dropped," she said casually, as if commenting on the volume of his screams or the size of his feet. Obligatory nurse/new dad small talk.

"That's normal then?"

"Sometimes they're just a bit shy."

My husband didn't mention it to me until we were safely stashed away in the recovery room. "She says they'll probably drop."

I had no reason to question it. For weeks, I'd been ogled in grocery store lines by middle-aged women telling me I'd "definitely dropped". Dropping, it seemed, was a natural step in the saga of human reproduction.

The doctor mainly affirmed the nurse's assessment. Most likely, this was a textbook case of cryptorchidism, the medical term for undescended testicles. However, he told us, ambiguous hardware sometimes signaled a condition called congenital adrenal hyperplasia. CAH was rare—worst-case scenario—but he wanted to order some tests, just to be safe.

The urine test was normal, his ultrasound came back negative (no uterus or ovaries, a good sign) but the final diagnostic—a blood test—would need to be completed after his newborn hormones had a chance to settle.

And so, three days later, numb and buzzing from exhaustion, we strapped him into the chasmic void of his car seat and drove to the address the nurse had written on our discharge papers.

The laboratory was the DMV of healthcare centers—the same sour, bleachy smell of a hospital, but missing the artificial floral arrangements and cheap watercolors. All business with no pretenses. The nylon lobby chairs lining the perimeter were filled with people glued to their phones, waiting to be checked for STDs and celiac disease and diabetes.

"They couldn't just get a sample from his heel at the hospital?" one of the phlebotomists asked when they called us back.

I shrugged. (We barely know how to fasten a diaper, I wanted to tell her.)

"We don't usually do arm draws at three days old," she said uneasily. "Try to avoid it as much as possible, anyway."

On the drive over, my husband had done his best to reassure me. "I'm sure it'll be quick and easy. They do it all the time."

I'd nodded, willing myself to believe him. But now, as I watched them place a rubber tourniquet over his bratwurst-sized bicep, doubts began to creep in.

They smeared the iodine (awkward small talk) and prodded the crook of his elbow (forced smiles). When the weapon was finally unsheathed, a needle as long as his middle finger, my whole body tensed.

The tech wielding it took a deep breath. "Alright. One, two, three."

Our son screamed. Not the "I'm alive!" howl from birth, triumphant and aware as he gulped his first lungfuls of oxygen, nor the hungry shrieks that had since been waking us at ungodly hours of the night. It was the scream of pain and fear, his first real taste of corporeal suffering.

Didn't get it. Let's try again. One, two, three. Still nothing. God, these veins are like strands of hair. So sorry little guy, hang in there just one more minute.

I was unprepared for my body's biological reaction, the fight and flight instinct to grab him from their arms and make a run for it. His cries pulsed through my veins, burrowed inside my bones.

And I swear to God, I could feel the needle.

It wasn't that I'd expected motherhood to be easy. The combined forces of pregnancy and childbirth (nausea, aching breasts, swift kicks to the cervix, jackhammer contractions, perineal tears, more blood than should ever come out of a single living organism) had adequately forewarned me. And to some degree, I knew what lie ahead. Grocery store tantrums and Sharpie on the walls. Phone calls from principals. Missed curfews. Wrecked cars.

What I hadn't expected was the jarring realization that there was no such thing as cutting the cord. I'd heard the snip, seen my husband's white-knuckled grip on the umbilical scissors with my own two eyes, but it had been a mirage. A clever illusion. From this point on I would feel, sometimes acutely, skinned knees and broken bones, recess betrayals, the sting of kindergarten bullies telling him his art was junk.

Eventually, there would be weightier sorrows. Debilitating fears. Broken hearts. Pain that would be felt in a million different ways.

It seemed like a revelation, but I knew the disclaimer had been there all along, written in fine print in the creases on my own mother's forehead.

A few months down the road, a urologist would find the missing testicles up near his hip bones, fish them down, and sew them into place. I would cry—for myself, but also for all the other parents in the lobby whose children did have CAH. For those waiting to hear if the tumor had been removed. If the bleeding had stopped. If the bone was set.

But in that bleak laboratory, three days a mother, past and future melted away, leaving only the moment they put my son back into my arms. His tiny, shuddering frame gradually melted into mine, and I savored the fleeting sensation of completeness, of relief, of the lost being found.

DW McKinney

Conducting Inventory

Jagged squares laid open-faced on the floor of my eldest daughter's bedroom. Peering across the room, I saw slender triangles too. Although innocuous in form, these black anomalies confounded me.

I had a very detailed accounting of all the things in our home. I mentally inventoried every gift or store-bought item along with the history that came with it. Our joys, tears, and sicknesses were engrained in our furniture, clothes, and cherished blankets as well. This knowledge became invaluable the moment my children began to ask, "Where's my _____?" I could tell you when and where an object was purchased and where it was located in our home. I was also acutely aware of their state of decline. Lately my sense of inventory had been disrupted by my eldest. She had been taking things of mine, moving the inventory around the home so to speak. She adopted my belongings as her own until she returned them—or I acquiesced and gifted them to her. Currently my colorful pens resided in the utensil well on her desk. My lip balm sat on her nightstand.

Standing in the doorway of my daughter's bedroom, I mentally scanned the house from top to bottom. I didn't know where these shapes should have been located. The more I thought about them, the more my head ached. I marched to the squares and triangles, then squatted to get a closer look. *Why did she put them there? Where did they come from?*

Intrusive thoughts wound around my confusion and squeezed. My imagination and anxiety transformed these unfamiliar shapes into objects that would harm my daughter the longer they remained on the floor, uncategorized.

Realization squelched the panic rising inside me. These intrusive thoughts were rooted in my worry for who my daughter was becoming and how I loved seeing myself in her, as well as how much I hoped to connect to her as she matured into a person who was more than me. When she was born, I had to reckon with the immediate cognitive dissonance of our difference. She was a biracial child born to a Black mother and a white father. If had been doing inventory at the time, I would have made note that there were three of us in the house then, one of us a copy of the others. I saw my eyes, nose, and ears on her face. I spent so much time—maybe too much—watching her when she was not looking, pasting the memory of my child-self onto her, finding the edges that aligned and the ones that did not. I wanted to make sure that I had not been subsumed. That I would not be forgotten later.

The more my eldest daughter grew, the more I peered into her visage to check that I was still there. To see what others only guessed: that I was her mother.

I dismissed my intrusive thoughts and picked the shapes off the floor. They flopped over my fingertips. They were just pieces of fabric. Recognition crackled like a lightning bolt from my head to my core. I knew where these shapes belonged—conducting inventory hadn't failed me.

I threw open the flimsy bedroom closet doors. Blankets crocheted by my friends, and gifted during my baby shower, were neatly stacked on the shelf. School uniforms and dresses from Target hung from the closet rod. On top of my daughter's dresser was a crumpled dress. I plucked it up between my thumb and index fingers. It was the new black dress I bought for her two days ago. She had cut up the sleeves.

Other shirts sat in a pile on the dresser top. Their sleeves were cut too. Flotsam littered the closet floor, and as I reached down, my hand wavered over a dark blue mass of fabric. My heart seized. It was my best dress. The only dress that still fit me. The dress I loved to wear to formal events with my husband. The dress I kept in the back half of my bedroom closet, accounted for. I did not know how I missed its absence except to think that it has been too long since we'd had someplace to go during the pandemic.

I picked up the dress, frantic, and examined every inch of it. I clutched the intact fabric to my chest and ran to my bedroom closet, where I slipped it on a hanger. As I placed the hanger on the closet rod, the dress shifted, exposing a curve of white plastic where the fabric parted by design. When worn, it gave a peekaboo effect on my shoulders. I laughed until I wept.

Any lingering thoughts of being forgotten quickly fell away. My daughter had been using my dress as a pattern to redesign her clothes, cutting up her sleeves to match mine. She had altered her own inventory, if ever so slightly, to resemble my own.

Ashley W. Cundiff

Thrive

I tried to talk myself out of having children. After all, when considered logically, it seemed there was no good reason for me to procreate, but several good ones not to—I shirk responsibility whenever possible, there is nothing remarkable about my DNA, and of course, there is the glaring, number one reason—the world seems to be sick, failing at an exponential pace. It made no sense for me to have children, but of course I have three. Because as much as my mind was convinced that children were not advisable, Mother Nature, or biology, or the human spirit, or some combination of all of these overthrew it. So, about eight years ago, I found myself talking my husband into having a child with a dogged optimism that defied all of the current realities of the time, a pursuit that resulted in my daughter's birth. Four years after that, despite circumstances that were even more disheartening, there I was lobbying for another. When that second child turned out to be two sons, there was no need to convince my husband or myself—we had enough. But the deed was done, and now I find myself the mother of three children, each one perfect both despite and because of the fact that they are mine.

Sometimes my divided spirit wrestles with the question of whether I should feel guilty for having children. On one hand, it would never occur to my human nature, which is self-serving, and simple, and thinks little of the future, to regret it. Because as it turns out, according to it, there is something remarkable about my DNA after all. There must be, because the world cannot turn without my children in it; the idea is simply inconceivable. But the more cerebral side of my spirit, the loftier side, tries to glimpse their lives in the future, and it is this part of me that wonders if what I have done is the right thing. Climate change, unrest, disease, a pulsing of evil in humanity…none of this is worthy of my children's lives. And sometimes, when I look at them in their great and innocent enthusiasm, I worry that before long they will find this world to be a great disappointment, and that maybe I should have left their gorgeous spirits to roam the cosmos, piercing space with their brilliant small lights.

I am not the pessimist that I may seem to be. I am, rather, a fierce optimist, perhaps even to the point of denial. I garden, after all—what could be more optimistic than burying hope in the ground with the assumptions that it will flourish and that you will be around to witness it? I admit, though, that I'm not a good gardener, but a reckless one who blindly flings seeds and bulbs everywhere, hoping that something will have the tenacity to live. Every year I have multiple failures in the garden—raccoons dig up my bulbs, cats use newly planted seed beds as litter boxes, deer eat much of what does grow, and by midsummer everything has gone to weeds. But still every spring I plant again. And there are small victories, though I can never quite pinpoint how they happen or why. At our old house, I had green beans and roses galore, though most everything else I planted there died. One year, I aced cucumbers, another, I had heaps of basil, though no tomatoes. What was probably my best crop was an unintentional one—we had a tradition of tossing old pumpkins and gourds into our wooded front yard once their season had passed, but it was only after a tornado destroyed much of these woods in the spring of 2019 that five years' worth of seeds felt the sun and germinated, creating a strange wonderland of vines which flowered in profusion and whose broad leaves grew to cover squash and gourds of all varieties. It is likely that the tornado, a weather event that was not considered a threat to our area a couple of decades ago, was at least partially a result of climate change. It exposed our home and our vulnerabilities in a way that we had not expected and to which we would have preferred to remain naïve. But it is certain that without the chaos of the tornado, these magical vines would never have sprung to life. If I have a prayer, it is this: let my children thrive as they did.

Those seeds, like my children, were tossed into an environment that was less than ideal, a place where darkness seemed to have the upper hand. They experienced unforeseen chaos, a shock of blinding reality, and it was then that they were forced into life. I am not prone to believe that spirits choose to born, at least I am not prone to believe that spirits choose to be born in any way that their earthly forms should be held accountable for. I make myself crazy believing that it is I who must take the credit or the fall for the lives of my children. I, so human, so lowly, who watched a pumpkin bounce down a hill ignorant to the fact that within it was new life that would appear only when the landscape surrounding it was destroyed. It was I who recklessly bore my children with an intense determination that all would be well. It is I who refuses to prophesy anything for the future but sun and seasons and growth, forever and ever. My accountability for my children's lives tortures me, yet…when I see a flower emerging from a haggard vine, still I am an optimist. How can I not be when right in front of me is something so determined to grow? How can I not be when somehow, in the dark, in the chaos of driving winds, my children have burst forth, not as vines, but as suns, their brilliant light commanding me to thrive?

CONTRIBUTORS' NOTES

Deborah Bacharach is the author of *Shake & Tremor* (Grayson Books, 2021) and *After I Stop Lying* (Cherry Grove Collections, 2015). Her poems, essays and book reviews have been published in *Poetry Ireland Review, Vallum, Cimarron Review,* and *Poet Lore* among many others. She has received a Best of the Net nomination, three Pushcart prize nominations and a Pushcart prize honorable mention. She teaches poetry workshops for children. Find out more about her at DeborahBacharach.com.

Subhaga Crystal Bacon's new book, *Transitory*, is forthcoming in the fall of 2023 from BOA Editions. She's the author of two previous collections, *Blue Hunger*, 2020, Methow Press, and *Elegy with a Glass of Whiskey*, BOA Editions, 2004. A Queer Elder, she lives, writes, and teaches rural north-central Washington on unceded Methow land. Her recent work appears or is forthcoming in *45th Parallel, Rogue Agent, The Indianapolis Review*, and *Rise Up Review*.

Jennifer Barber's most recent collection is *The Sliding Boat Our Bodies Made* (The Word Works, 2022). Previous collections include *Works On Paper, Given Away*, and *Rigging The Wind.* She is the co-editor, with Jessica Greenbaum and Fred Marchant, of the anthology *Tree Lines: 21st American Poems* (Grayson Books, 2022). She lives in the Boston area.

Carrie Bennett is a Massachusetts Cultural Council Artist Fellow and author of three poetry books, *Biography of Water, The Land Is a Painted Thing, Lost Letters* and *Other Animals*, and several chapbooks from dancing girl press. Her poems have appeared in numerous journals, including *Boston Review, Caketrain, Denver Quarterly,* and *jubilat*. She holds an MFA from the Iowa Writers' Workshop and teaches writing at Boston University. She lives with her family in Somerville, MA.

Margo Berdeshevsky, NYC born, writes in Paris. Recent books are *Before The Drought*, Glass Lyre Press, (finalist, National Poetry Series), and *Kneel Said the Night* (a hybrid book in half-notes) Sundress Publications. *It Is Still Beautiful To Hear The Heart Beat* is forthcoming from Salmon Poetry. Berdeshevsky is also the author of *Between Soul & Stone* and *But a Passage in Wilderness* Sheep Meadow Press, and *Beautiful Soon Enough*, winner of the Ronald Sukenick Innovative Fiction Award. Other honors: Grand Prize, Thomas Merton Poetry of the Sacred, Robert H. Winner Award, Poetry Society of America. http://margoberdeshevsky.com

Watched by crows and friend to salamanders, Lisa Creech Bledsoe is a hiker, beekeeper, and writer living in the mountains of Western North Carolina. She is the author of two full-length books of poetry, *Appalachian Ground* (2019), and *Wolf Laundry* (2020), as well as a chapbook, *Reflection With Crow* (2022). She has poems out in *Chiron Review, Otoliths*, and *Quartet*, among others.

Mary Bonina's two poetry collections are *Living Proof* and *Clear Eye Tea*. She is also the author of *My Father's Eyes: A Memoir* as well as a completed novel, *My Way Home,* being submitted to publishers. A fellow of the Virginia Center for the Creative Arts and recipient of a Moulin a Nef (VCCA-France) residency, she earned her MFA at Warren Wilson College. Learn more more about her and her work at http://www.marybonina.com

Mary Lou Buschi (She/Her) holds an MFA in poetry from the MFA Program for Writers at Warren Wilson College and a Master of Science in Urban Education from Mercy College. Her poems have appeared in literary journals such as *Radar, The Laurel Review, The Shore, Bluestem* and are forthcoming in *Ploughshares, West Trestle*, and *Sweet.* Her second full length collection, *Paddock*, was published by Lily Poetry Review Books in 2021.

Kevin Carey's books include: *The Beach People* (2014), *The One Fifteen to Penn Station* (2012), *Jesus Was a Homeboy* (2016) which was an Honor book for the Paterson Literary Prize, and *Set in Stone* (2020). His crime novel, *Murder in the Marsh*, from Darkstroke Books, was released in 2020. A new novel, *Junior Miles and the Junkman*, will be published in September of 2023 from Fitzroy Books, an imprint of Regal House Publishing. Kevincareywriter.com

Robert Carr is the author of three collections of poetry: *Amaranth*, published by Indolent Books; *The Unbuttoned Eye*, and *The Heavy of Human Clouds*, from 3: A Taos Press. His poetry appears in many journals and anthologies, and he is the recipient of a 2022 artist residency at Monson Arts, sponsored by the Maine Writers and Publishers Alliance. Additional information can be found at robertcarr.org

M.P. Carver is a poet and visual artist from Salem, MA. M.P. serves as Director of the Massachusetts Poetry Festival and teaches at Salem State University. She is miCrO-founder of *Molecule*; a tiny lit mag, former Poetry Editor of *Soundings East*, and an Editor at YesNo Press. Her work has appeared most recently in *9x5*, an anthology of 5 new voices by Only Human Press. Her chapbook, *Selachimorpha*, was published by Incessant Pipe in 2015.

Sofia Chapman completed a BA (Hons) in Modern Languages in Tasmania before running away with the accordion to play on a theatre barge in France. Sofia returned to Australia to study playwriting and is now a professional accordionist with the band Vardos and co-produces queer plays at La Mama Theatre. 'The Four Accordionists of the Apocalypse' received the 2012 Melbourne Fringe 'Best Emerging Writer' Award. Sofia's stories, poems, cartoons, short films and audiobooks appear internationally.

Eileen Cleary is the author of *Child ward of the Commonwealth* (Main Street Rag Press, 2019), which received an honorable mention for the Sheila Margaret Motton Book Prize and *2 a.m. with Keats* (Nixes Mate, 2021). In addition, she co-edited the anthology *Voices Amidst the Virus*, the featured text at the 2021 Michigan State University Filmetry Festival.

Ashley W. Cundiff is a musician, usually disgruntled but occasionally inspired adjunct instructor, mother of three gorgeously wild children, and writer-by-night who is thrilled to have recently completed her first novel. She lives with her family in the woods of southwestern Virginia; you can find her at www.thedomesticwilds.com.

Julia Kolchinsky Dasbach, Ph.D. (www.juliakolchinskydasbach.com) emigrated from Ukraine as a Jewish refugee at age six. She is author of three collections: *The Many Names for Mother*; *Don't Touch the Bones*; and *40 WEEKS* (YesYes Books, 2023), in which "Week 38: Leek" first appeared. Her poems have appeared in *POETRY, Ploughshares*, and *APR*. She teaches Creative Writing at Hendrix College and in fall 2023, Julia will join Denison University as Assistant Professor of English/Creative Writing.

Ariane Dreyfus is a widely published French poet with 16 collections to her credit. "Inside" is from *The Last Children's Book*. Elaine Terranova has published seven collections and two chapbooks. Her eighth collection, *Rinse*, will appear in 2023.

Merridawn Duckler is the author of *Interstate* (dancing girl press) and *Idiom* (Washburn Prize, Harbor Review.) New work in *Seneca Review, Women's Review of Books, Interim, Posit, Plume*. Winner of the 2021 Beullah Rose Poetry Contest. She's an editor at *Narrative* and the philosophy journal *Evental Aesthetics*.

Suzanne Edison's first full length book, *Since the House Is Burning*, was published by MoonPath Press in 2022. Her chapbook, *The Body Lives Its Undoing*, was published in 2018. Poetry can be found in: *Bracken; Michigan Quarterly Review; Lily Poetry Review; Whale Road Review; Scoundrel Time; JAMA; SWWIM;* and elsewhere. She is a 2019 Hedgebrook alum and teaches at Richard Hugo House in Seattle and through UCSF.

Jennifer R. Edwards' debut poetry collection is *Unsymmetrical Body* (Finishing Line Press, 2022). She's a Pushcart Prize nominated poet & preschool speech-language pathologist living in Concord, NH with her family. Her poems won (2022) and were honorably mentioned (2020) for the New England Poetry Club Amy Lowell Prize. Her poems appear in many anthologies & literary mags including *Terrain, Tiny Spoon, Remington Review, Snapdragon, Literary Mama.* Twitter @Jennife00420145 See her work at https://linktr.ee/JenEdwards

Kelley Engelbrecht is an MFA candidate in creative nonfiction at Columbia College where her work interrogates womanhood and traditional gender roles. She lives in Chicago with her husband, daughter and cat.

Natalie Shaw Evjen has a predilection toward things that make her cry, which she blames on her Enneagram number. (She's a hard Four.) Her work has been featured in *Dialogue Journal, Sixfold Journal,* and was nominated for a Pushcart Prize by *Brilliant Flash Fiction.* A Utah native, she currently lives with her husband and two children in Lincoln, Nebraska where she writes, teaches, and cheers for the Huskers.

Lupita Eyde-Tucker writes and translates poetry in English and Spanish. She's the winner of the 2021 Unbound Emerging Poet Prize. Recent work appears in *Women's Voices for Change, Yemassee, Rattle, [PANK], Night Heron Barks,* and *Jet Fuel Review.* Lupita is an MFA candidate in Poetry at the University of Florida, and has received support from Bread Loaf Writers Conferences, the Kentucky Women Writers Conference, and New York Summer Writers Institute. Read more poems: www.NotEnoughPoetry.com

Sandra Fees has been published in *SWWIM, Harbor Review, Nimrod, River Heron Review, Witness,* and other journals. She was a 2022 contest finalist in *Sweet: A Literary Confection* and semifinalist in *Crab Creek Review.* The author of *The Temporary Vase of Hands* (Finishing Line Press, 2017), she lives in southeastern Pennsylvania.

Jessica Femiani received her PhD in English and creative writing at Binghamton University (SUNY). Her poems and essays have been published in the *Paterson Literary Review, #MeToo Anch'Io,* and *Labor.* She is a member of the Working Class Studies Association and lives in Binghamton, New York.

Brandel France de Bravo is the author of *Provenance* (Washington Writers Publishing House poetry prize winner), *Mother, Loose* (Accents Publishing, Judge's Choice Award) and the editor of a bilingual anthology of contemporary Mexican poetry. Her poems and essays have appeared in *Alaska Quarterly Review,* the *Cincinnati Review,* *The Georgia Review, Gulf Coast, Poet Lore,* the *Seneca Review* and elsewhere. She teaches a meditation program developed at Stanford University called Compassion Cultivation Training.©

Elizabeth Cranford Garcia's work has or will soon appear in journals such as *Tar River Poetry, CALYX, Dialogist, SoFloPoJo, Mom Egg Review, Psaltery & Lyre,* and *SWWIM*, and has been nominated for the Pushcart Prize and Best of the Net. Her chapbook, *Stunt Double*, was published in 2016 through Finishing Line Press. She is the current Poetry Editor for *Dialogue: a Journal of Mormon Thought,* a Georgia native and mother of three.

Violeta Garcia-Mendoza is a Spanish-American poet, writer, and photographer. She is a member of Carlow University's Madwomen in the Attic Writing Workshops. Her poetry has been nominated for a Pushcart Prize and Best of the Net, and has won a Sustainable Arts Foundation grant. Violeta lives with her family in western Pennsylvania.

Marie Gauthier is the author of *Leave No Wake* (Pine Row Press, 2022). Her poems have appeared in *Poetry Northwest, Sugar House Review, The West Review,* and elsewhere. She works for Pioneer Valley Books, runs the Collected Poets Series in Shelburne Falls, Mass., where she lives with her family, and serves on the executive boards of the League of Women Voters of Franklin County and Massachusetts.

Jennifer Georgescu is an interdisciplinary artist based in Basel, Switzerland. Her self-reflective projects focus on language, relationships, mythologies and control. She is a three time finalist for Critical Mass, Photolucida, was awarded the John Chervinsky Scholarship, through the Griffin Museum of Photography, and received the William Male Foundation Grant in 2019, and 2020.
Recent exhibitions include the Athens Phot Festival, Blue Sky Gallery, Startup Art Fair LA, and others.

Joan Kwon Glass is the mixed-race, Korean American author of *Night Swim* (Diode Editions, 2022) and three chapbooks. She serves as Editor-in-Chief for *Harbor Review,* as a Brooklyn Poets Mentor and is a proud Smith College graduate. Her work has been nominated for the Pushcart Prize and Sundress Anthology Best of the Net. Joan's poems have been published or are forthcoming in *Prairie Schooner, RHINO, Rattle, The Rupture, Dialogist* and elsewhere. She lives in Connecticut.

Laura Goldin is a publishing lawyer in New York. Five of her recent poems appear in the Spring 2023 issue of *The Brooklyn Review,* and one is forthcoming in *Driftwood Press 2024 Anthology.* Other poems have been published or are forthcoming in *Bellevue Literary Review, Apple Valley Review, The Comstock Review, Gargoyle Magazine, One Art,* and *The Spoon River Poetry Review*, among others.

Robin Gow (they/he/ze) is a trans poet and YA/MG author. They are the author of several poetry collections, an essay collection, and a YA novel in verse, *A Million Quiet Revolutions.* Gow's poetry has recently been published in *POETRY, New Delta Review,* and *Washington Square Review.*

Pat Hale's publications include the poetry collections, *Seeing Them with My Eyes Closed* and *Composition and Flight.* Her prize-winning poems appear in *Calyx, Connecticut River Review, Uppagus,* and many other journals, and are anthologized in *Forgotten Women, Waking Up to the Earth: Connecticut Poets in a Time of Global Climate Crisis,* and elsewhere. She lives in Connecticut in a little house surrounded by tall trees, and serves on the board for the Riverwood Poetry Series.

Shannon Elizabeth Hardwick's work has appeared, or is forthcoming, in *Gulf Coast, Salamander Magazine, Frontier Poetry, MAGMA Poetry, The Texas Observer, Four Way Review, The Missouri Review,* and *Passages North,* among others. Hardwick serves as the Editor-in-Chief at *The Boiler.*

Marie Harris, New Hampshire Poet Laureate 1999-2004, is a writer, teacher, and editor. She has served as writer-in-residence in elementary and secondary schools, and is the author of five books of poetry, including *Desire Lines* from Hobblebush Books (2019). Her books for children include *G Is For Granite: A New Hampshire Alphabet, Primary Numbers: A New Hampshire Number Book,* and a picture book, *The Girl Who Heard Colors.* She lives in Asheville, NC.

Katie Hartsock's second poetry collection is *Wolf Trees* (2023, Able Muse Press). Her work has recently appeared or is forthcoming in *Kenyon Review, Ecotone, Missouri Review, Beloit Poetry Journal,* and *Plume.* She is an associate professor of English at Oakland University and lives in Ann Arbor, Michigan, with her husband and sons.

Sarah Herrington is a poet, essayist and teacher. Her work has appeared in *The New York Times, LA Times, Tin House, Slice* and other spots. She lives online at www.sarahherrington,com.

KateLynn Hibbard's books are *Sleeping Upside Down*, *Sweet Weight*, and *Simples*, winner of the 2018 Howling Bird Press Poetry Prize. Some journals where her poems have appeared include *Barrow Street, Ars Medica, Nimrod,* and *Prairie Schooner*. Editor of *When We Become Weavers: Queer Female Poets on the Midwest Experience*, she teaches at Minneapolis College and lives with many pets and her spouse Jan in Saint Paul. katelynnhibbard.com.

Melissa Joplin Higley toured internationally as a sound engineer with Yo-Yo Ma and the Silk Road Ensemble and Disney's The Lion King North American Tour. Her poems appear in *FERAL, The Night Heron Barks, Writer's Digest,* and elsewhere. She holds an MFA from Sarah Lawrence College and co-facilitates the Poetry Craft Collective. She lives in Mamaroneck, NY with her husband and son. Visit her at: melissajoplinhigley.com.

Rae Hoffman Jager is the author of *American Bitch*. Rae's poetry has appeared in a wide variety of online and print magazines, including *Contrary Mag, Atticus*, and *Honey Lit*. She has work forthcoming in *New York Quarterly*. Rae holds a BA from Warren Wilson College and an MFA from Wichita State University. When she is not writing, publishing, and teaching yoga, she is spending time with her spouse, daughter, and two old dogs.

Crystal Karlberg is a Library Assistant at her local public library and a speaker for Greater Boston PFLAG.

Tina Kelley's *Rise Wildly* appeared in 2020 from CavanKerry Press, joining *Abloom & Awry, Precise,* and *The Gospel of Galore*, a Washington State Book Award winner. She reported for *The New York Times* and wrote two nonfiction books. Her poems have appeared in *Poetry East, Southwest Review, Prairie Schooner,* and *The Best American Poetry 2009*. She is the senior education reporter for NJ.com. She and her husband have two children and live in Maplewood, NJ.

Claire Keyes is the author of two collections of poetry: *The Question of Rapture* and *What Diamonds Can Do*. Her chapbook, *Rising and Falling*, won the Foothills Poetry Competition. A second chapbook, *One Port*, was recently published by Derby Wharf Books. She is Professor emerita at Salem State University and her poems and reviews have been published recently in *Valparaiso Poetry Review, Turtle Island*, and *Tipton Poetry Journal*. She lives in Marblehead, Massachusetts.

Debbie Koenig is the author of the cookbook *Parents Need to Eat Too* (William Morrow). Her bylines have appeared in *Eating Well, Cooking Light, Parenting, The New York Times*, the annual *Best Food Writing* anthology, and elsewhere. She lives in Queens, NY, with her husband, their rainbow-haired teenage son, and two very large cats.

Andrea Krause lives in Portland, Oregon with her family. Her work has been published in: *The Penn Review, The Shore, Moist Poetry Journal,* and elsewhere. She introverts on Twitter at @PNWPoetryFog.

Anaïs La Rocca is a writer and director. Her work has appeared in The New York Times, Raven's Perch, as well as other literary magazines. She won an International Motion Arts Award for her short film *Good Bones,* based on the poem by acclaimed poet Maggie Smith. You can find her work at www.anaislarocca.com

Danielle Lemay is a poet and a scientist. Her poetry has been nominated for Best of the Net and has appeared in *SWWIM Every Day, California Quarterly, San Pedro River Review, The Blue Mountain Review,* and many other publications. She lives in central California with her wife, two children, and six chickens. More at www.DanielleLemay.com.

Barbara Lock is a writer, editor, teacher, and physician. Her writing appears in *Westchester Review, Superstition Review, STORY, The Forge,* and elsewhere. There's more about her at barbaralock.com.

Tarisa A.M. Matsumoto lives in a tiny house with four humans and four canines. She loves all things soccer and pretending the world isn't falling to pieces. She also assumes that people are honest and kind, which has gotten her into occasional trouble. She teaches writing at Highline College in south Seattle.

DW McKinney is a writer and editor based in Nevada. Her work has appeared or is forthcoming in *Los Angeles Review of Books, Ecotone, The Normal School, Hobart Pulp, Barrelhouse,* and *Hippocampus Magazine,* among others. She is a nonfiction editor for *Shenandoah* and editor-at-large for *Raising Mothers.* Say hello at dwmckinney.com.

Livia Meneghin (she/her) is the author of *Honey in My Hair* and *GASHER* reviews. She's the winner of Breakwater Review's 2022 Peseroff Prize, a Writers' Room of Boston Fellowship, and The Academy of American Poets' 2020 University Prize. Her writing has found homes in *Solstice Lit, Thrush,* and elsewhere. She earned her MFA at Emerson College, where she now teaches writing and literature, and is Program Coordinator for EmersonWRITES. She is a cancer survivor.

Chloe Yelena Miller lives in Washington, D.C., with her family. She is the author of *Viable* (Lily Poetry Review Books, 2021) and *Unrest* (Finishing Line Press, 2013). Chloe teaches writing at American University and University of Maryland Global Campus, as well as privately. chloeyelenamiller.com / @ ChloeYMiller

Gloria Monaghan is a Professor at Wentworth University. Her poems have appeared in *Alexandria Quarterly, NPR, Poem-a-Day, Lily Poetry Review, Mom Egg Review, Quarte*t and *River Heron* among others. She has been nominated twice for the Pushcart Prize, as well as the Massachusetts Book Award, and the Griffin Prize. Her sixth book, *Cormorant on the Strand,* 2023, has been published with Lily Poetry Review.

Abby E. Murray is the editor of *Collateral,* a literary journal concerned with the impact of violent conflict and military service beyond the combat zone. She teaches rhetoric in military strategy to Army War College fellows at the University of Washington. After serving as poet laureate for the city of Tacoma, Washington, she recently (and temporarily) relocated to Washington DC, where her spouse works in the Pentagon.

Loretta Oleck is a Pushcart Poetry Prize nominee, Westchester County Poet Laureate finalist, and creative artist with works published worldwide. Her photography has been published in the *Adirondack Review, Picayune Magazine, Switched on Gutenberg, Subterranean Quarterly, 580 Split, Dirty Chai, Elohi Gadugi Journal, Rogue Agent, Red Dash* (cover photo), *Cactus Heart* (cover photo), and exhibited in numerous galleries including in a digital exhibition at the Louvre. She is also a mother and grandmother.

Dayna Patterson is a Thea-curious recovering Mormon, fungophile, macrophotography enthusiast, and textile artist. She's the author of *Titania in Yellow* (Porkbelly Press, 2019) and *If Mother Braids a Waterfall* (Signature Books, 2020). Honors include the Association for Mormon Letters Poetry Award and the 2019 #DignityNotDetention Poetry Prize judged by Ilya Kaminsky. Her creative work has appeared recently in *EcoTheo, Kenyon Review,* and *Whale Road Review.* "Gertrude on arte materna" was originally published in *O Lady Speak Again* (Salt Lake City: Signature Books, 2023), 92. daynapatterson.com.

Anne Elezabeth Pluto grew up in Brooklyn, NY before it was cool. She is Professor of Literature and Theatre at Lesley University in Cambridge, MA where she is the artistic director of the Oxford Street Players. She is one of the founders and editors of *Nixes Mate Review* and Nixes Mate Books. Her latest poetry collection is *The Deepest Part of Dark,* Unlikely Stories Press, NOLA.

Jennifer Pons is a high school literature and writing teacher in Portland, Oregon. Her poems have appeared in *Across the Margin, Whale Road Review, EKSTASIS Magazine, Ninth Letter, Psaltery & Lyre, Opt West,* and *CutBank Flash Poetry and Prose Online*, where she was named a finalist for the Patricia Goedicke Prize in Poetry. Her manuscript "Locusts and Wild Honey" was named a finalist for the Pamet River Prize 2020.

Kyle Potvin's debut full-length poetry collection is *Loosen* (Hobblebush Books, 2021). Her chapbook, *Sound Travels on Water*, won the Jean Pedrick Chapbook Award. Her poems have appeared in *Bellevue Literary Review, Tar River Poetry, Ecotone, The New York Times*, and others. She is a peer reviewer for *Whale Road Review*. Kyle lives on the Seacoast of New Hampshire.

Kimberly Ann Priest is the author of *Slaughter the One Bird*, finalist for the American Best Book Awards, and chapbooks *The Optimist Shelters in Place, Parrot Flower,* and *Still Life*. She is an associate poetry editor for *Nimrod International Journal of Prose and Poetry* and assistant professor at Michigan State University.

Jessica Purdy holds an MFA from Emerson College. Her poems have appeared or are forthcoming in many journals including *The Night Heron Barks, Lily Poetry Review, SoFloPoJo, One Art, Museum of Americana,* and *Harpy Hybrid*. She is the author of the chapbook *Learning the Names* (Finishing Line Press) and two books of poems, *STARLAND* and *Sleep in a Strange House* (Nixes Mate Books). The latter was a finalist for the NH Literary Award for poetry.

Kimberly Ramos is a queer Filipina writer from Southern Missouri. They dream of becoming a cryptid and haunting the Midwest. For now, they enjoy watching rom coms with their mother. Their chapbook *Alive, Today, Again!* was recently named first runner-up of the 2022 Flume Press Chapbook Contest, to be published in 2023. You can read more of their work at https://kimramoswrites.carrd.co/

Glenis Redmond is a performance poet. Her books include *Backbone* (Underground Epics, 2000), *Under the Sun* (Main Street Rag, 2002), and *What My Hand Say* (Press 53, 2016), *The Listening Skin* (Four Way Books), and *Praise Songs for Dave the Potter, Art by Jonathan Green* (University of Georgia Press). Glenis received the highest arts award in South Carolina, the Governor's Award and was inducted into the South Carolina Academy of Authors in April 2022.

Jeff Rivers is an African-American, self-taught visual artist, designer, and community advocate who works to empower minority groups through social impact art programs and street art. Jeff Rivers' practice is a mixed media blend of painting and drawing that combines the figurative with abstract landscapes. Rivers uses fabric in his paintings to 'dress' the figure to create life-size representations of people documented from his daily experience. Memory and a sense of place are conjured through these figures. The texture of the fabric invites the viewer to engage with the work in close physical touch and intimacy, however the anonymity of the figures accentuates a sense of isolation and emotional detachment.

Tessa Ellison Rossi is a writer, teacher, recovering attorney, and associate managing editor at *Variant Lit* who holds an MFA from Sarah Lawrence College and a third dan in taekwondo. Words in *Red Ogre Review* and its anthology, Grey Sparrow Press, and *Roi Faineant*. She's @TRossiWriter.

Karen Elizabeth Sharpe is from Westminster, Massachusetts. Karen is a poetry editor at the *Worcester Review*, and her poems have recently appeared in *Main Street Rag, West Trade Review, Catalyst, the Mizmor Anthology, Mason Street Review*, among others. Karen has been nominated for a Pushcart Prize, Best of the Net, and her chapbook, *Prayer Can Be Anything*, has recently been accepted for publication by Finishing Line Press.

Martha Silano's most recent collection is *Gravity Assist* (Saturnalia Books, 2019). Previous collections include *Reckless Lovely* and *The Little Office of the Immaculate Conception,* also from Saturnalia Books. Martha's poems have recently appeared in *Alaska Quarterly Review, Southern Indiana Review,* and *Colorado Review*, among others. Honors include the *North American Review's* James Hearst Poetry Prize and *The Cincinnati Review's* Robert and Adele Schiff Award. Martha teaches at Bellevue College. Her website is available at marthasilano.net.

Dorsía Smith Silva is a four-time Pushcart Prize nominee, Best of the Net finalist, Best New Poets nominee, Cave Cavem Poetry Prize Semifinalist, Obsidian Fellow, and Full Professor at the University of Puerto Rico. Her poetry has recently been published or is forthcoming in *Waxwing, The Minnesota Review, The Offing,* and *Shenandoah.* She is the author of *Good Girl* (micro-chapbook), editor of *Latina/ Chicana Mothering*, and the co-editor of seven books. She posts on Twitter @DSmithSilva.

Anne Starling was born in California and now lives in Florida. She has owned a used book store and done social work for a living. Her work has appeared in *Southern Review, Missouri Review, Carolina Quarterly, Rattle* and other journals.

Meghan Sterling's work is forthcoming in *The Los Angeles Review, Rhino Poetry, Nelle, Colorado Review, Poetry South,* and many others. Her poetry collection, *These Few Seeds* (Terrapin Books), came out in 2021. Her chapbook, *Self-Portrait with Ghosts of the Diaspora* (Harbor Editions) her collection, *Comfort the Mourners* (Everybody Press) and her collection, *View from a Borrowed Field,* which won Lily Poetry Review's Paul Nemser Book Prize, are forthcoming in 2023. Read her work at meghansterling.com.

Darlene Taylor is a Washington, DC-based multidisciplinary artist and writer. She is the Aminah Robinson Writer-in-Residence at the Columbus Museum of Art and recipient of fellowships from the D.C. Commission for the Arts. Through experiences in national politics, global corporate communications, and nonprofit service, Taylor has been an advocate for creating access and opportunity for underrepresented communities. She is a lecturer at Howard University and serves on the board of The Clifton House.

Pramila Venkateswaran, poet laureate of Suffolk County, Long Island (2013-15) and co-director of Matwaala: South Asian Diaspora Poetry Festival, is the author of many poetry volumes, the most recent being *We Are Not A Museum* (Finishing Line Press, 2022). She has performed her poetry internationally, including at the Geraldine R. Dodge Poetry Festival. An award-winning poet, she teaches English at SUNY, Nassau. She is the President of NOW, Suffolk, New York.

Lauren Walke is an illustrator living amongst the folklore and trees of Appalachia. She creates art based on ritual, folklore, and the aspects that call (loudly) to her. Lauren's work is amplified and enhanced by her focus on daily rituals, seeking for moments of magic in life alongside her family, an unending consumption of books and music, and by tending the shrines of tiny treasures and plants around her house.

Annelies Zijderveld's poetry has been published in *Acentos Review*, the *Scapegoat Review, ethelzine,* the *New Republic*, and others. She is co-editor of interviews at *the Rumpus*, a contributing editor to *Harpy Hybrid Review*, and holds an MFA in poetry from New England College.

MOM EGG REVIEW

Mom Egg Review Issues Available

Vol. 20 "Mother Figures"	2022, Paper, 132 pp. $18
Vol. 19	2021, Paper, 141 pp. $18
Vol. 18 "Home"	2020, Paper, 139 pp. $18
Vol. 17	2019, Paper, 117 pp. $18
Vol. 16 "Play and Work"	2018, Paper, 118 pp. $18
Vol. 15	2017 Paper, 123 pp. $18
Vol. 14 "Change"	2016 Paper, 128 pp. $18
Vol. 13 "Compassionate Action"	2015 Paper, 154 pp. $18
Vol. 12	2014 Paper, 150 pp. $18
Vol. 11 "Mother Tongue"	2013 Paper, 125 pp. $18
Vol. 10 "The Body"	2012 Paper, 120 pp. $18
Vol. 9	2011 Paper, 120 pp. $18
Vol. 8 "Lessons"	2010 Paper, 120 pp. $18
Vol. 7	2009 Paper, 124 pp. $18

*Plus US shipping $3.50 for the first book, $1.00 for each additional book.

Subscribe to *MER*

US shipping is free for subscription copies!

One year $18
Two years $36

Order on the web at
www.merliterary.com (Click "Shop")

or mail your order with a check to

Mom Egg Review
PO Box 9037
Bardonia, NY 10954

Contact: themomegg@gmail.com
Email for info about discounts for quantity purchases and for classroom use, or for out-of-country shipping. MER is also available through EBSCO.

www.ingramcontent.com/pod-product-compliance
Lightning Source LLC
LaVergne TN
LVHW081320110826
845149LV00006B/1553
* 9 7 8 0 9 9 1 5 1 0 7 9 5 *